Learning Responsive Data Visualization

Master the art of building responsive visualizations on the Web

Christoph Körner

PUBLISHING

BIRMINGHAM - MUMBAI

Learning Responsive Data Visualization

First published: March 2016

Production reference: 1180316

Published by Packt Publishing Ltd.
Livery Place
35 Livery Street
Birmingham B3 2PB, UK.

ISBN 978-1-78588-378-1

www.packtpub.com

Credits

Author
Christoph Körner

Reviewer
Sébastien Fragnaud

Commissioning Editor
Wilson D'souza

Acquisition Editor
Reshma Raman

Content Development Editor
Sachin Karnani

Technical Editor
Gebin George

Copy Editor
Yesha Gangani

Project Coordinator
Nikhil Nair

Proofreader
Safis Editing

Indexer
Monica Ajmera Mehta

Graphics
Disha Haria

Production Coordinator
Nilesh Mohite

Cover Work
Nilesh Mohite

About the Author

Christoph Körner, CTO and lead developer at GESIM, a start-up company, is a passionate software engineer, web enthusiast, and an active member of the JavaScript community with more than 5 years of experience in developing customer-oriented web applications. He is the author of *Data Visualizations with D3 and AngularJS* and is currently pursuing his master's degree in Visual Computing at Vienna Institute of Technology.

I want to thank my close friends, Firat Özdemir and Vidor Kanalas, for their continuous support and help, as well as my boss and colleague, Dietmar Wiegand, for supporting all my ideas and dreams. I also want to thank my girlfriend, Laura Andrea Rojas Padilla, who has always inspired, motivated, and supported me, as well as the whole team at Pack Publishing for believing in me and supervising me during the last 6 months.

About the Reviewer

Sébastien Fragnaud is a frontend engineer who works at Metamarkets. He creates beautiful UIs out of beautiful mockups. Before this, he worked for several different companies, but his focus was always the same: presenting data in a meaningful manner.

Deeply fond of reusable code, he's the author of n3-charts, a JavaScript library that provides an easy way to manipulate charts in AngularJS applications.

www.PacktPub.com

eBooks, discount offers, and more

Did you know that Packt offers eBook versions of every book published, with PDF and ePub files available? You can upgrade to the eBook version at www.PacktPub.com and as a print book customer, you are entitled to a discount on the eBook copy. Get in touch with us at customercare@packtpub.com for more details.

At www.PacktPub.com, you can also read a collection of free technical articles, sign up for a range of free newsletters and receive exclusive discounts and offers on Packt books and eBooks.

https://www2.packtpub.com/books/subscription/packtlib

Do you need instant solutions to your IT questions? PacktLib is Packt's online digital book library. Here, you can search, access, and read Packt's entire library of books.

Why subscribe?

- Fully searchable across every book published by Packt
- Copy and paste, print, and bookmark content
- On demand and accessible via a web browser

Table of Contents

Preface

Data visualizations are the best way to understand complex information and data. The human brain perceives visual information easily; it can make connections and is able to understand the complete process easier than without visualizations.

I am always delighted with the positive feedback from users whenever they understand a complex system easily by looking at a data visualization, instead of going through explanatory text and raw data. With the power of the Web and modern browsers, I can share these visualizations with everyone and make them interactive and animated.

To power cross-browser interactive visualization, I didn't want any compromise with regards to performance, debugging, quality, and interactivity, which led me to SVG. After deciding for SVG, I looked for a framework for SVG transformations giving raw access to all its underlying standards while also providing a rich set of visualization features - the D3.js library provides all of these.

D3.js is a visualization toolkit that facilitates the generation and manipulation of web-based vector graphics and provides full access to underlying SVG standards. Moreover, animations and interactive visualizations change the way users perceive web applications, and D3.js offers everything you need to make a visualization interactive out of the box.

While this has been working for the last few years, I realized that users are increasingly accessing visualizations with their mobile devices, though mostly through smartphone and tables. On most tablets, visualizations looked good, though interactions did not work anymore. Smartphone users experienced this as well when they tried to zoom into a browser but it somehow interfered with the zoom of the visualization and randomly toggled interactive features instead. For me, this was the sign I needed to fix the problem.

With the rise of responsive web design, there were already plenty of ideas for creating cross-browser and cross-platform applications that adapt to a user's device, screen size, and resolution. Apart from this, modern browsers already provide solid CSS and JavaScript functionality to implement responsive designs for all kinds of web applications.

The only logical step for me was to combine rich tools in order to create responsive applications and introduce the same ideas into data visualizations. I want my visualizations to adapt to the user's device, screen size, and resolution while providing cross-platform interactivity for mouse and touch gestures. In this book, I will share my knowledge, experience, and best practices on responsive data visualizations with you.

What this book covers

Chapter 1, Getting Started with Responsive Design, Bootstrap, and D3.js, gets you on track with today's concepts, technologies, and frameworks to create responsive applications.

Chapter 2, Creating a Bar Chart Using D3.js and SVG, helps you get started with `D3.js` and its concepts. You will learn how to draw points, shapes, and simple bar charts by the end of this chapter.

Chapter 3, Loading, Filtering, and Grouping Data, guides you so that you can get the maximum information out of real-world data.

Chapter 4, Making the Chart Responsive Using Bootstrap and Media Queries, goes through all of the steps needed to make visualizations responsive and adapt them to user devices.

Chapter 5, Building Responsive Interactions, teaches you to add truly responsive interactions to your visualization, which also makes these great to use on user devices.

Chapter 6, Designing Transitions and Animations, teaches you to make a visualization appealing to look at by adding gorgeous transitions or custom animations.

Chapter 7, Creating Maps and Cartographic Visualizations Using GeoJSON, helps you get started with geographic data processing and then visualize this data in cartographic visualizations.

Chapter 8, Testing Responsive Visualizations, shows you how to test responsive visualizations both manually and in an automated manner, and covers both unit and end-to-end testing.

Chapter 9, Solving Cross-Browser Issues, helps you avoid the most common pitfalls when dealing with cross-browser compatibility issues for responsive visualizations.

What you need for this book

The first thing you need to get started with is a web browser and text editor, such as Sublime Text or Atom. Then, you need to install node.js (http://nodejs.org/) — which already includes the npm package manager — and the bower package manager (http://bower.io/). I will walk you through the installation of the required packages in the corresponding chapters.

For examples that require you to load data from your local hard drive, I would recommend that you install the http-server module (https://www.npmjs.com/package/http-server) to run all the examples from a local web server. An Internet connection is only required to install tools and libraries but not to run the examples.

Who this book is for

This book is intended for data scientists, developers, and motivated beginners to implement custom responsive data visualizations using vector graphics. Whether you already know a bit about SVG and vector graphics in a browser or you have never used any visualization library before, you will be able to master the data-driven techniques of D3. In either case, this book will get you up and running as quickly as possible and also challenges you if you have already worked with D3.

Conventions

In this book, you will find a number of text styles that distinguish between different kinds of information. Here are some examples of these styles and an explanation of their meaning.

Code words in text, database table names, folder names, filenames, file extensions, pathnames, dummy URLs, user input, and Twitter handles are shown as follows: "We can use the d3.text function and parse the dataset on our own."

A block of code is set as follows:

```
var lines = data.split(/\n/g)
  .map(function(line) {
    return line.split(/[-"]/g);
  });
```

When we wish to draw your attention to a particular part of a code block, the relevant lines or items are set in bold:

```
// Parsing strings to numbers
var i = parseInt("5.0", 10);
var f = parseFloat("3.8");

// Short notation
var s = "932.2";
var j = +s;
```

Any command-line input or output is written as follows:

```
bower install d3
```

New terms and **important words** are shown in bold. Words that you see on the screen, for example, in menus or dialog boxes, appear in the text like this: "As we can see in the following figure, the test passes and Karma shows a green **SUCCESS** status."

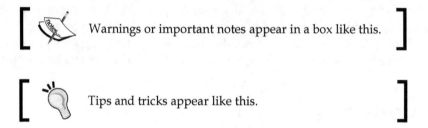

Warnings or important notes appear in a box like this.

Tips and tricks appear like this.

Reader feedback

Feedback from our readers is always welcome. Let us know what you think about this book—what you liked or disliked. Reader feedback is important for us as it helps us develop titles that you will really get the most out of.

To send us general feedback, simply e-mail feedback@packtpub.com, and mention the book's title in the subject of your message.

If there is a topic that you have expertise in and you are interested in either writing or contributing to a book, see our author guide at www.packtpub.com/authors.

Customer support

Now that you are the proud owner of a Packt book, we have a number of things to help you to get the most from your purchase.

Downloading the example code

You can download the example code files for this book from your account at http://www.packtpub.com. If you purchased this book elsewhere, you can visit http://www.packtpub.com/support and register to have the files e-mailed directly to you.

You can download the code files by following these steps:

1. Log in or register to our website using your e-mail address and password.
2. Hover the mouse pointer on the **SUPPORT** tab at the top.
3. Click on **Code Downloads & Errata**.
4. Enter the name of the book in the **Search** box.
5. Select the book for which you're looking to download the code files.
6. Choose from the drop-down menu where you purchased this book from.
7. Click on **Code Download**.

Once the file is downloaded, please make sure that you unzip or extract the folder using the latest version of:

- WinRAR / 7-Zip for Windows
- Zipeg / iZip / UnRarX for Mac
- 7-Zip / PeaZip for Linux

Downloading the color images of this book

We also provide you with a PDF file that has color images of the screenshots/ diagrams used in this book. The color images will help you better understand the changes in the output. You can download this file from https://www.packtpub. com/sites/default/files/downloads/LearningResponsiveDataVisualization_ ColoredImages.pdf.

Errata

Although we have taken every care to ensure the accuracy of our content, mistakes do happen. If you find a mistake in one of our books—maybe a mistake in the text or the code—we would be grateful if you could report this to us. By doing so, you can save other readers from frustration and help us improve subsequent versions of this book. If you find any errata, please report them by visiting `http://www.packtpub.com/submit-errata`, selecting your book, clicking on the **Errata Submission Form** link, and entering the details of your errata. Once your errata are verified, your submission will be accepted and the errata will be uploaded to our website or added to any list of existing errata under the Errata section of that title.

To view the previously submitted errata, go to `https://www.packtpub.com/books/content/support` and enter the name of the book in the search field. The required information will appear under the **Errata** section.

Piracy

Piracy of copyrighted material on the Internet is an ongoing problem across all media. At Packt, we take the protection of our copyright and licenses very seriously. If you come across any illegal copies of our works in any form on the Internet, please provide us with the location address or website name immediately so that we can pursue a remedy.

Please contact us at `copyright@packtpub.com` with a link to the suspected pirated material.

We appreciate your help in protecting our authors and our ability to bring you valuable content.

Questions

If you have a problem with any aspect of this book, you can contact us at `questions@packtpub.com`, and we will do our best to address the problem.

1
Getting Started with Responsive Design, Bootstrap, and D3.js

The best way to understand data is to visualize it and explore it using an interactive visualization. In this book, we are going to build such an interactive visualization (actually many of them) using the latest techniques and web technologies. To make the information accessible across all devices, we are going to make the visualizations responsive. However, before we can start, we need to understand what this actually means. We also want to reuse some existing frameworks to not just do a great job but also work in an efficient way.

This chapter serves as an introduction to the methods, technologies, and frameworks that we will use throughout the book, and it will help you understand why we are using them to create data visualizations and how they work together.

In this chapter you will learn the following:

- What exactly is Responsive Design and how can it be applied to create visualizations that work across all different screen sizes and resolutions
- What is a Media Query and how it can be used to design visualizations for various devices
- Why and how we use Bootstrap to build the visualization on existing components
- Why we use vector graphics, such as SVG, for the web
- Why we use D3.js for data manipulation and graphics creation

First, you will learn about *Responsive Design* and how it can be used to design a visualization for various screen sizes and resolutions. Then, we will discuss the importance of some key technologies such as CSS3 (especially Media Queries) and HTML5 (especially the viewport meta tag).

In the following chapter, we will get acquainted to the popular CSS and HTML framework called **Bootstrap**. Don't worry if you have never heard about it; it helps us to build the application on the existing and well-tested components, such as **grids** and **LESS** Media Queries.

In the last section of this chapter, you will learn about **Scalable Vector Graphics (SVG)** in the browser; and you will understand why and when it is great to use vector graphics for visualizations. Then, we will see a brief introduction to D3.js, which is a versatile JavaScript library for data transformations and graphics generation. At the end of this chapter, you will understand why SVG is a great choice for designing interactive responsive visualizations for the web.

What is Responsive Design?

Responsive Design is a method for designing applications that can adapt their appearance and behavior to the user's device. It makes the application look and feel good across all different devices, and most often, it makes them usable on all devices.

An important paradigm in Responsive Design is to use relative dimensions instead of fixed widths, heights, margins, paddings, and font sizes throughout all the application to adapt the design to the various types of devices.

For web browsers, Responsive Design was enabled through CSS3 and HTML5 features, such as Media Queries, the viewport meta tag, and new dimension units.

Conditional CSS with Media Queries

Media Queries were introduced in CSS3 as a more flexible extension of Media Types. They allow the developer to apply conditional CSS styles only when a statement (a so-called query) matches a certain CSS property (so-called Media Features) and a Media Type. A typical Media Query has the following structure:

```
@media [Media Type [and|not|only]] (Media Feature) {
    ...
}
```

Here is a small selection of properties that can be used as Media Features:

- `width`, `min-width`, and `max-width`
- `height`, `min-height`, and `max-height`
- `device-width`, `min-device-width`, and `max-device-width`
- `device-height`, `min-device-height`, and `max-device-height`
- `resolution`, `min-resolution`, and `max-resolution`

 A complete list of Media Features and Types can be found on MDN at `https://developer.mozilla.org/de/docs/Web/CSS/Media_Queries/Using_media_queries`.

In Responsive Design, we are mostly interested in querying the `min-width` or `max-width` property to apply different styles to devices that have different widths.

Let's see an example where we can apply a different background color depending on the minimal width of the browser window:

```
div {
    background-color: blue;
}
@media screen and (min-width: 992px) {
    div {
        background-color: red;
    }
}
```

In the preceding example, all the `div` elements in the page have the background color `red` as long as the browser window's width is larger or equal to, 992 px (see the following figure):

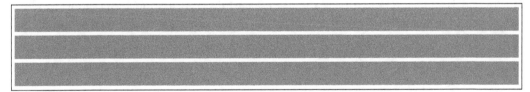

Browser window width larger than 992px

Once the window width is smaller than 992 px, the background color of the `div` elements jumps to `blue` (see the following figure):

Browser window with width smaller than 992px

As we can see in the following figure, Media Queries are supported across all major browsers and Internet Explorer starting from version 9:

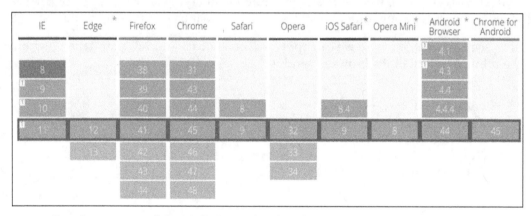

Cross-browser compatibility Media Queries from http://caniuse.com/#feat=css-mediaqueries

Understanding Breakpoints

In Responsive Design, we call a **state** when a certain layout and Media Query is active, and we call a **breakpoint** the transition from one state to another.

Let's look at an example. First, we define some screen dimensions for the following devices:

- `<768px` is for phones
- `768px-992px` is for tablets
- `992px-1200px` is for desktops
- `≥1200px` is for large devices and TVs

Create a CSS snippet using Media Queries for these device dimensions:

```
/* phones, default no query */
/* tablets */
@media (min-width: 768px) { ... }
/* desktops */
@media (min-width: 992px) { ...}
/* large devices */
@media (min-width: 1200px) { ... }
```

In the preceding code, we defined four states with three breakpoints between these states where each state corresponds to a typical screen dimension and device type.

We can also see these breakpoints by reducing the size of a browser window while looking at a responsive web page; we observe how the design breaks at a certain width of the browser window. In the following figure, the breakpoint is visualized as a dashed line, showing the moment when one state breaks into a new one:

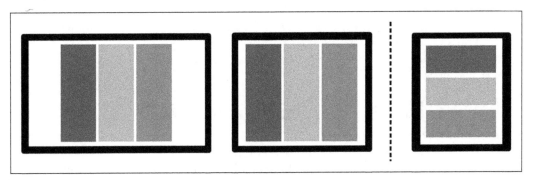

Breakpoint in Responsive Design

We can observe the same effect when we look at the Google Plus web page in the following figure. In the first two figures, the size of browser window changes, but the three-column layout stays the same. In the third image, the design breaks into a new layout with only two columns:

Breakpoints of the Google Plus page

Having the right viewport

Across mobile and desktop devices, there exists a vast variety of different pixel densities and screen resolutions. Displays with much higher resolution would render pages much smaller than displays with a lower resolution; this immediately leads to readability problems. To prevent this effect and fit bigger pages into smaller screens, a virtual window — the so-called `viewport` (the visible area of a web page) — was introduced. This allowed websites to render in the correct pixel resolution and scale to the full device width for maximal accessibility; however, developers had no control over this device-specific setting. Later, in HTML5, the `viewport meta` tag was introduced in order to give developers full control over these viewport settings.

Today, a mobile-optimized application usually defines the following `viewport` tag in the `head` section of the web page to render the website normally and scale the content to the width of the device:

```
<meta name="viewport" content="width=device-width, initial-scale=1">
```

 More information about all the valid viewport options can be found on MDN at `https://developer.mozilla.org/en-US/docs/Mozilla/Mobile/Viewport_meta_tag`.

Relative Units – %, REM, and EM

When dealing with Responsive Design, it is always a good idea to use relative units to describe the element's dimensions based on its parent element. Thus, when the parent container changes the size, all children elements adapt their sizes accordingly.

The most popular unit for relative dimensions is `%`, which defines the dimension based on a certain percent of the next absolute positioned parent element.

However, there are more useful units to describe relative dimensions; for example, the following two are based on the font-size:

- `em`: This is relative to the font size of the element
- `rem`: This is relative to the font size of the root element

These units have a big advantage; they are affected by the changes of the font-size setting in the browser. A simple example can be the adaption of the paddings when the user increases the font size of the browser.

A short summary and explanation of all different CSS units can be found on MDN at `https://developer.mozilla.org/de/docs/Web/CSS/length`.

Designing for mobile devices first

Responsive applications should look and feel great (or work at all) on a huge number of devices with a huge number of different screen sizes and resolutions; they usually run on mobile devices as well as big TV screens. Thus, in the beginning of a project, every developer has to choose an approach to design the responsive application to master this transition; in general, we distinguish between the following methods:

- Mobile first
- Desktop first

In the desktop first method, we design for desktop devices and mouse input first, then we adjust and scale the design down for mobile devices and touch interactions. This often results in a web application with a reduced functionality for mobile devices due to a much smaller screen dimension and the lack of touch support.

In the mobile first method, we design for mobile devices and touch interactions first, and then we adjust and scale the design up for bigger devices and mouse interactions. This approach makes sure that mobile devices support a complete set of features, which can even be used on desktop clients.

Both methods are equally correct, accepted, and popular nowadays. The only exception is that mobile first became a buzzword due to an increase of mobile devices accessing the web during the previous years. Throughout the book, we will choose a mobile first approach and design for mobile devices and touch support. However, we will, of course, extend the visualizations to support mouse input and bigger screens. That's what the responsive design is all about.

Bootstrap – a popular mobile first CSS framework

If we want to create responsive mobile first web applications, we usually don't want to start from zero and re-implement common patterns and components; we would rather want to reuse some well-tested, existing components.

Bootstrap is a very popular HTML and CSS framework built by former Twitter employees for easy, fast, and modern frontend development; it provides loads of responsive CSS and LESS layouts as well as a huge collection of HTML and JavaScript components. Thanks to its MIT license, it can be used in open source and commercial software.

The current stable version 3.3.5 includes LESS styling with these features:

- Containers and grids (static and fluid)
- Responsive helpers (hiding and showing elements on different breakpoints)
- LESS mixins and variable declarations
- Styles for common components such as forms, input fields, and tables
- Icons, HTML, and JavaScript components

 A complete list of features can be found on the Bootstrap website at http://getbootstrap.com/.

The new version 4 (which is currently in the alpha stage) will be shipped with SASS layouts and loads of other great features and improvements:

 There also exists an official fork for the SASS precompiler on GitHub at https://github.com/twbs/bootstrap-sass.

- All units are in rem an em
- A new xl grid tier is added
- Optional flexbox support
- A Reboot module is available to reset default browser styles

 A complete list of new features can be found on the Bootstrap blog at http://blog.getbootstrap.com/2015/08/19/bootstrap-4-alpha/.

Throughout this book, we will use Bootstrap 3.3.5 version (with LESS) for all the examples and explanations if they are not stated differently. We will also give some hints about the latest version where it is appropriate.

Including Bootstrap

Make sure you have the Bower package manager installed; this can be done by running the following command from the terminal:

```
npm install -g bower
```

 More information about the Bower package manager can be found on its website at `http://bower.io/`.

Throughout this book, we will make use of only the CSS components of Bootstrap and thus we only need to include the `bootstrap.css` file to our project. There are multiple ways of doing so:

- Use the package manager called `bower` (recommended) — First, fetch the library by running the following command from the terminal — **bower install bootstrap#3.3.5**. Then, link the minified CSS file from the **bower_components/** directory in the `head` section of the web page: `<link rel="stylesheet" href="bower_components/bootstrap/dist/css/bootstrap.min.css">`.

- Use a **Content Delivery Network (CDN)**, such as MaxCDN (this requires an active Internet connection while developing). Simply include the minified CSS file from the CDN in the `head` section of the web page: `<link rel="stylesheet" href="https://maxcdn.bootstrapcdn.com/bootstrap/3.3.5/css/bootstrap.min.css">`.

- Manually, download the 3.3.5 release from GitHub (`https://github.com/twbs/bootstrap/releases`) and unzip it into the **libs/** directory. Then, link the minified CSS file from the **libs/** directory in the `head` section of the web page: `<link rel="stylesheet" href="libs/bootstrap/dist/css/bootstrap.min.css">`.

I strongly recommend using the `bower` package manager to manage your frontend dependencies (or similar ones, such as `npm` or `component`). However, in the examples of this book, we will link Bootstrap directly from MaxCDN for simplicity reasons; therefore, all examples in the source of the book require an active Internet connection.

Finding additional resources

The ultimate resource for Bootstrap is the documentation that can be found at `http://getbootstrap.com/getting-started/`. Here, you will also find examples and templates using the Bootstrap framework.

For more detailed information and examples, I recommend reading the *Unraveling Bootstrap 3.3* book by *Istvan Novak*.

Understanding grid layouts

A popular component to organize elements in an application or visualization is a grid layout. For responsive design in particular, we are mostly interested in grid layouts that adapt their columns to the screen resolution of the client. In the following figure, there's an example of a responsive grid layout with three columns per row on a desktop device and one column per row on a mobile device:

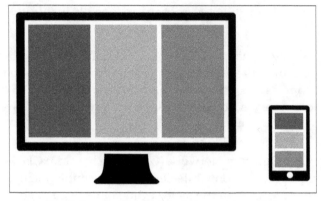

Simple Responsive grid, left: desktop, right: mobile

We then distinguish two different types of responsive grids that adapt the number of columns to the screen resolution of the client:

- *Normal* grids with a fixed width per breakpoint (see following figure on the left)
- *Fluid* grids that always scale to the full width of the current breakpoint (see the following figure on the right)

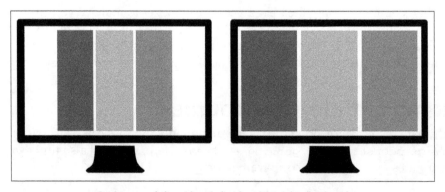

Grid types—left: grid with fixed width, right: fluid grid

It's actually quite simple to build a grid system yourself; let's first take a look at how to create a fluid grid layout, and afterwards, we will better understand how we can use Bootstrap components to get things done quickly and properly.

If we think about a grid as a (flexible) table layout, we need two basic components: rows and columns. A popular approach is to use the *12-column grid* where we divide the width of a row into 12 columns and define column combinations that sum up to the full width of 12. The following figure illustrates some of these combinations: 12 columns of width 1, 6 columns of width 2, 4 columns of width 3, and so on. Also other combinations that sum up to 12 are allowed, such as 2, 6 and 4 or 1, 10 and 1 and many more.

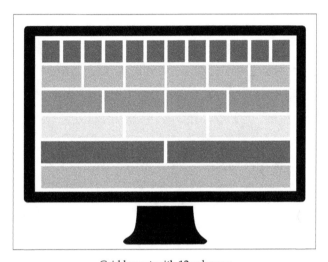

Grid layout with 12 columns

Let's start and build the .row class that spans to the full width of the parent element:

```
.row {
  position: relative;
  width: 100%;
}
```

Next, we want to create column classes .col-1, .col-2, ..., and .col-12 that define the width of the column in the percent relative to the width of the row. We define a text wrap with the float attribute and add padding for the cells. The float attribute indicates that the block element should not appear in the original flow but "float" on the left side. By doing so, we align the elements in the same line instead of placing them into the normal text flow:

```
[class*="col-"] {
  float: left;
```

```css
    padding: 1em;
  }
  .col-1 {
    width: 8.33333333%;
  }
  .col-2 {
    width: 16.66666667%;
  }
  .col-3 {
    width: 25%;
  }
  .col-4 {
    width: 33.33333333%;
  }
  .col-5 {
    width: 41.66666667%;
  }
  .col-6 {
    width: 50%;
  }
  .col-7 {
    width: 58.33333333%;
  }
  .col-8 {
    width: 66.66666667%;
  }
  .col-9 {
    width: 75%;
  }
  .col-10 {
    width: 83.33333333%;
  }
  .col-11 {
    width: 91.66666667%;
  }
  .col-12 {
    width: 100%;
  }
```

In the preceding code, we see that we can use the wildcard attribute selector called [class*="col-"] to select all the columns at once (all the classes that contain the col- letters). The widths have to be defined as per column type.

The only problem in the previous example is that, by default (box-sizing: content-box), the padding size of the columns adds up with the width property to determine the computed width of the element. The total width of all elements plus the padding sizes would give a number bigger than 100% of the parent element. Using the box-sizing: border-box property, we can disable this behavior and the computed width of the element equals the width property:

```
[class*="col-"] {
  -webkit-box-sizing: border-box;
  -moz-box-sizing: border-box;
  box-sizing: border-box;
}
```

Finally, we need to clear the text-wrapping property of the columns after each row. We can do this by adding a clearfix pseudo element after each .row class:

```
.row:after {
  content: " ";
  display: block;
  clear: both;
}
```

This is already a nice implementation of a basic grid system. Let's test this layout and create an HTML page with the following content:

```
<div class="row">
  <div class="col-1">.col-1</div>
  <div class="col-1">.col-1</div>
  <div class="col-1">.col-1</div>
  <div class="col-1">.col-1</div>
  <div class="col-1">.col-1</div>
  <div class="col-1">.col-1</div>
  <div class="col-1">.col-1</div>
  <div class="col-1">.col-1</div>
  <div class="col-1">.col-1</div>
  <div class="col-1">.col-1</div>
  <div class="col-1">.col-1</div>
  <div class="col-1">.col-1</div>
</div>
<div class="row">
  <div class="col-2">.col-2</div>
  <div class="col-2">.col-2</div>
  <div class="col-2">.col-2</div>
  <div class="col-2">.col-2</div>
  <div class="col-2">.col-2</div>
```

```
    <div class="col-2">.col-2</div>
  </div>
  <div class="row">
    <div class="col-3">.col-3</div>
    <div class="col-3">.col-3</div>
    <div class="col-3">.col-3</div>
    <div class="col-3">.col-3</div>
  </div>
  <div class="row">
    <div class="col-4">.col-4</div>
    <div class="col-4">.col-4</div>
    <div class="col-4">.col-4</div>
  </div>
  <div class="row">
    <div class="col-6">.col-6</div>
    <div class="col-6">.col-6</div>
  </div>
  <div class="row">
    <div class="col-12">.col-12</div>
  </div>
```

If we add a little bit of coloring (the complete example can be found in the code files of the book) and open the HTML page in the browser, we get a layout similar to the following figure:

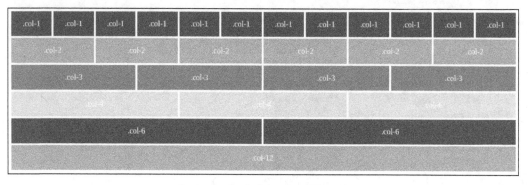

Browser output of simple grid layout

Let's take a look at the responsive grid system provided by Bootstrap, which looks very similar to the one that we have just created. Bootstrap defines Media Queries for four device types (the so-called grid tiers) and their corresponding typical viewport widths (in pixel) for the responsive breakpoints:

- Default for extra small devices (xs) such as phones

- ≥768px for small devices (sm) such as tablets and phones in landscape mode

- ≥992px for medium devices (md) such as desktops

- ≥1200px for large devices (lg) such as large desktops and TVs

> In Bootstrap 4, the breakpoints are now defined in em units:
>
> - Default for extra small devices
> - ≥34em for small devices
> - ≥48em for medium devices
> - ≥62em for large devices
> - ≥75em for extra large devices

The grid requires three different components:

- It requires a container element with the class called .container for fixed widths or .container-fluid for fluid containers

- It requires a row element with the class .row

- It requires one or more column elements:
    - .col-xs-1, .col-xs-2, ..., .col-xs-12
    - .col-sm-1, .col-sm-2, ..., .col-sm-12
    - .col-md-1, .col-md-2, ..., .col-md-12
    - .col-lg-1, .col-lg-2, ..., .col-lg-12

> Bootstrap 4 adds another .col-xl-* class for extra large devices.

Let's take a look at some code. First, we need to include the Bootstrap CSS to the header of the web page:

```
<!DOCTYPE html>
<html>
  <head>
    <link rel="stylesheet" href="https://maxcdn.bootstrapcdn.com/
bootstrap/3.3.5/css/bootstrap.min.css">
    <title>Simple Grid System</title>
    ...
  </head>
  <body>
    ...
  </body>
</html>
```

Now, we can add the grid layout according to the previous example, but this time, we need to wrap it in a fluid container:

```
<div class="container-fluid">
  <div class="row">
    <div class="col-lg-1">.col-lg-1</div>
    <div class="col-lg-1">.col-lg-1</div>
    ...
  </div>
  <div class="row">
    ...
  </div>
</div>
```

If we open the web page and look at the output of the web browser, we see an example similar to the following figure:

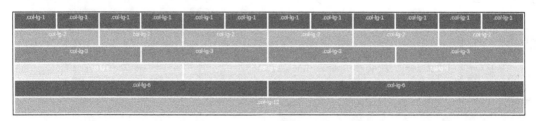

Browser output of grid layout with Bootstrap

We remark that the preceding figure looks very similar to the grid layout that we created in the beginning of this section. The only small difference in the code was the `.container` element to wrap the rows and the usage of the `.col-lg-*` classes. However, Bootstrap's grid is responsive, and the columns are arranged according to the breakpoints and the browser width. If we reduce the size of the browser window smaller than 1200px, we see that the grid jumps into a different layout. We can see this effect in the following figure:

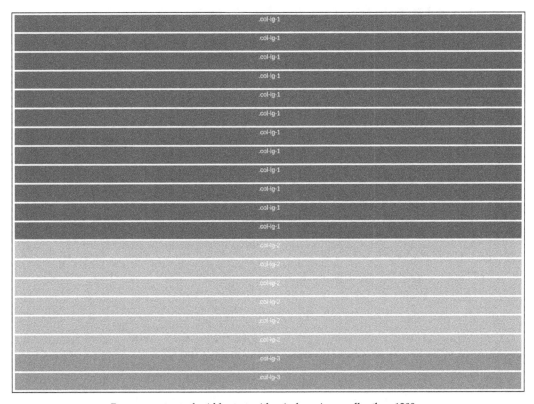

Browser output of grid layout with window size smaller than 1200px

The reason for this is that the browser window is no longer in the state of a very large device (greater than 1200px) and has jumped to a smaller state. Therefore, the `col-lg-*` columns are not applied anymore, and they appear in the full width of the row. We can now start to define certain column combinations to create a flexible responsive grid:

```
<div class="container-fluid">
  <div class="row">
    <div class="col-lg-3 col-md-6 col-sm-12"></div>
    <div class="col-lg-3 col-md-6 col-sm-12"></div>
    <div class="col-lg-3 col-md-6 col-sm-12"></div>
```

```
      <div class="col-lg-3 col-md-6 col-sm-12"></div>
    </div>
    <div class="row">
      ...
    </div>
  </div>
```

Hiding elements on different screen resolutions

Bootstrap also provides very handy and responsive utility classes to hide elements on certain browser widths. The classes are named according to the Media Query breakpoints:

- `.hidden-xs`
- `.hidden-sm`
- `.hidden-md`
- `.hidden-lg`

Hiding an element on a phone in portrait mode is as simple as adding a class to the element; let's take a look at the following example:

```
<ul class="nav">
  <li><a href="#menu">Menu</a></li>
  <li class="hidden-xs"><a href="#link">Link</a></li>
</ul>
```

The classes for showing elements on certain browser widths come for each breakpoint in three different variations depending on the CSS `display` property of the element:

- `.visible-*-block`
- `.visible-*-inline`
- `.visible-*-inline-block`

> The reason for these additional types is undesired line breaks and behaviors that occur when the `display` mode changes from `none` to `block`. Therefore, Bootstrap forces the user to specify the `display` property via the class name.

For these three blocks, all the breakpoint classes are available:

- `.visible-xs-*`
- `.visible-sm-*`
- `.visible-md-*`
- `.visible-lg-*`

Displaying an element only on a specific device width is also very simple:

```
<ul class="nav">
  <li><a href="#menu">Menu</a></li>
  <li class="visible-xs-block"><a href="#link">Link</a></li>
</ul>
```

 Bootstrap 4 provides only the `.hidden-*-down` and `.hidden-*-up` classes across all the breakpoints to the hide elements of certain device types.

Using Bootstrap's Media Queries in LESS

Bootstrap's stylesheet is written in LESS and we can make use of the predefined breakpoints and Media Queries easily.

 LESS is a CSS-like preprocessor language used to write stylesheets that support nesting, variables, functions, mixins, and much more. LESS files are compiled to CSS files during the development via the LESS compiler. If you've never heard about LESS, it is a good time to check it out via `http://lesscss.org/`.

Make sure you have the LESS compiler installed; this can be done by running the following command from the terminal:

```
npm install -g less
```

First, we create a `style.less` file and import Bootstrap's `variables.less` file at the beginning of the file. This enables us to reuse Bootstrap's declarations for colors, dimensions, and configurations throughout this file:

```
/* style.less */
@import "bower_components/bootstrap/less/variables.less";
```

Now, we can use Bootstrap's Media Query breakpoints in our LESS file. Let's add some device-specific padding to all the `div` containers:

```less
/* Extra small devices */
/* No media query since this is the default in Bootstrap */
div {
  padding: 4em;
}

/* Small devices */
@media (min-width: @screen-sm-min) {
  div {
    padding: 8em;
  }
}

/* Medium devices */
@media (min-width: @screen-md-min) {
  div {
    padding: 16em;
  }
}

/* Large devices */
@media (min-width: @screen-lg-min) {
  div {
    padding: 24em;
  }
}
```

Now, we use the LESS compiler to compile the stylesheet with CSS by running the following command in the terminal:

`lessc style.less style.css`

The resulting CSS looks similar to this:

```css
/* Extra small devices */
/* No media query since this is the default in Bootstrap */
div {
  padding: 4em;
}
/* Small devices */
@media (min-width: 768px) {
  div {
```

```
      padding: 8em;
    }
  }
/* Medium devices */
@media (min-width: 992px) {
  div {
    padding: 16em;
  }
}
/* Large devices */
@media (min-width: 1200px) {
  div {
    padding: 24em;
  }
}
```

Perfect! This means that we can now use the predefined breakpoints in our LESS styles.

Sometimes, it is also necessary to limit your styles to a narrow set of devices. Therefore, one can also use the `max-width` Media Queries in LESS. Again, the following code snippet is taken from the Bootstrap documentation at `http://getbootstrap.com/css/#grid-media-queries`:

```
@media (max-width: @screen-xs-max) { ... }
@media (min-width: @screen-sm-min) and (max-width: @screen-sm-max) {
... }
@media (min-width: @screen-md-min) and (max-width: @screen-md-max) {
... }
@media (min-width: @screen-lg-min) { ... }
```

This can be useful when we want to define styles for a single device type rather than all the devices with a screen width greater than or equal to the defined one.

Vector graphics in the browser with SVG

Now, it is time to create our first visualization. In HTML5, we have plenty of options to create graphics in the browser itself:

- Canvas API (or using, for example, `Paper.js`, `Processing.js`, and more)
- WebGL API (or using, for example, `Three.js`, `Pixi.js`, and more)
- SVG specification (or using for example `RaphaëlJS`, `D3.js`, and more)

To better understand which technology suits the best for our purpose of implementing responsive visualizations, we need to take a closer look and discuss their advantages and disadvantages.

Raster/Pixel graphics with Canvas

Canvas is a JavaScript API used to create *Raster Graphics* (often called *Pixel Graphics*) in the browser. As we can see in the following figure, it is supported in all major browsers and Internet Explorer starting from version 9:

> You can find detailed information about the Canvas API on MDN at https://developer.mozilla.org/en/docs/Web/API/Canvas_API.

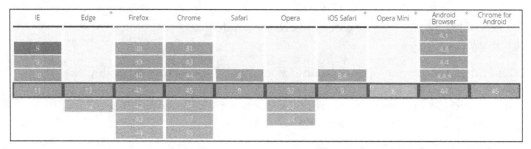

Cross-browser compatibility Canvas from http://caniuse.com/#feat=canvas

A Pixel Graphic is an image that contains all the information about the color of each pixel of the image for a certain resolution. Let's assume we have an image with 8 x 8 pixels where each of these 64 pixels contains the information about its color; we draw a circle in this image:

```
<canvas id="canvas"></canvas>
<script>
  var canvas = document.getElementById("canvas");
  var ctx = canvas.getContext("2d");
  var centerX = 10, centerY = 10, radius = 10;
  ctx.beginPath();
  ctx.arc(centerX, centerY, radius, 0, 2 * Math.PI, false);
  ctx.fillStyle = "red";
  ctx.fill();
</script>
```

In the following figure, one can see how the so-called rasterization process defines which pixels of this image gets colored (pixels in the blue region) for the circle shape and which pixels stays transparent (pixels in the white region):

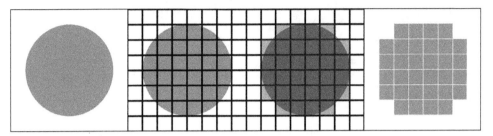

Rasterization of a 8 x 8 pixel circle shape

If we display this image with a high resolution (see the following figure at the left), we see a small circle with crisp edges. On the other hand, if we zoom into the image, we see a very pixelated 8 x 8 pixel image (see the following figure on the right); this effect is the direct cause of the resolution-dependent rasterization process:

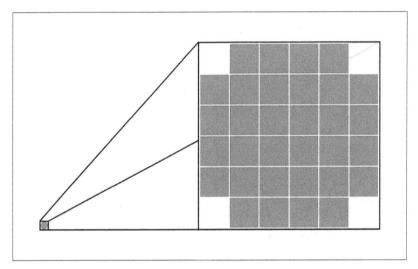

Pixel graphic, left: high resolution, right: zoomed

This effect makes it really difficult to use Pixel Graphics for Responsive Design; we have to always generate and reload our visualization for the current resolution and screen size.

Another drawback is that the final image is composed of pixels, which make it very difficult to attach event listeners, such as `mouseover` or `click` events, to certain components of the image. The reason for this is that there are no shapes or components encoded in the image but only color values for each pixel.

Hardware-accelerated Pixel Graphics with WebGL

WebGL is a JavaScript API based on OpenGL ES 2 to create hardware-accelerated 3D Pixel Graphics in the browser. This technology is very powerful and allows access to the client's GPUs via so-called Shaders; the final visualization is exposed in the browser via the Canvas element. However, browser support is not very good, as we can see in the following figure; mobile devices support the API only partially and Internet Explorer only from version 11.

 You can find more detailed information about the WebGL API on MDN at `https://developer.mozilla.org/en/docs/Web/API/WebGL_API`.

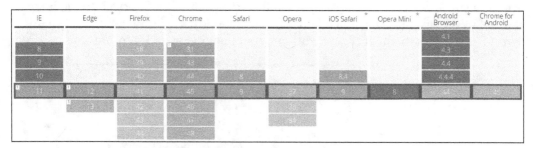

Cross-browser compatibility WebGL from http://caniuse.com/#feat=webgl

Due to WebGL's use of the Canvas element, it doesn't solve any of the limitations of Pixel Graphics that we discussed in the Canvas section. Thus, we will look at a different type of image representation next.

Vector graphics with SVG

SVG is an XML specification used to create and compose Vector Graphics. Thanks to HTML5, these graphics can simply be embedded into an HTML page, rendered and displayed perfectly sharp by the browser in every screen resolution. As we can see in the following figure, cross-browser compatibility is very good across all the major browsers and Internet Explorer starting from version 9:

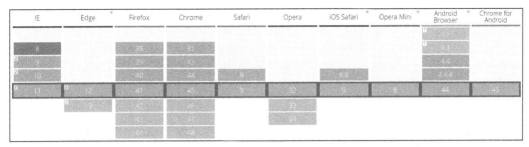

Cross-browser compatibility SVG from http://caniuse.com/#feat=svg

Vector Graphics are images where all the information about the image is encoded as numerical expressions of geometric shapes (such as rectangles, circles, ellipses, paths, and texts) of the elements of the image. The browser always uses this information to draw and render the graphic in the best resolution possible. In the following figure, we can see a Vector Graphic of a circle with a high resolution, whereas on the right, we see a zoom of the image. It's easy to see that the zoomed image is displayed with perfectly crisp edges; this effect of lossless scaling results from the resolution-dependent rendering of the browser.

 You can find detailed information about the SVG specification on the W3 website: `http://www.w3.org/Graphics/SVG/`.

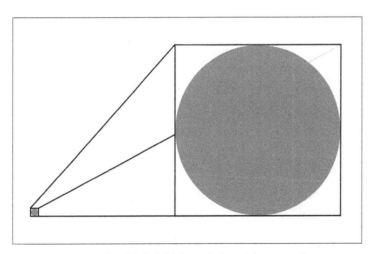

Vector Graphic, left: high resolution, right: zoomed

More advantages result from the fact that the visualization's elements are simply embedded in the HTML page. Now, we can easily attach native JavaScript event listeners, such as the `mouseover` or `click` events, on every component of the graphic and use CSS to style them together with the rest of the application.

Another great benefit is that we can simply look into the Developer Console of the web browser, play around, and debug the visualization. We can click on each element of the image to see its attached event handlers, and we can modify the CSS styling in real time. Anyone who has ever dealt with OpenGL or WebGL debugging will agree that this is a comfort that you can't miss while developing visualizations for the web.

Now, we already have many arguments in favor of using SVG for responsive cross-browser visualizations:

- Simple debugging because the source code of the graphic is simply embedded in the HTML document
- Sharp rendering on all screen resolutions because the browser renders the graphic according to the client's screen resolution
- Cross-browser compatibility in all major browsers
- Styling the visualization with CSS
- Native JavaScript event handlers can be attached to all elements of the image
- Debugging and live editing of the visualization in the Developer Tools

Creating graphics with D3.js

D3.js (abbreviation for Data-Driven Documents) is a JavaScript library built by Mike Bostock and other members of the Stanford Visualization Group for DOM manipulation, data transformation, and graphic creation. It uses a jQuery-like, data-driven approach and leverages all the capabilities of modern browsers and underlying web standards (such as HTML, CSS, and SVG).

D3.js is open source and hosted on GitHub (https://github.com/mbostock/d3) under a slightly modified BSD 3-clause license; therefore, it can be used in open source and commercial products without being required to release any modifications. GitHub itself uses D3.js to visualize the contribution history of repositories.

Throughout this book, we will use the stable version 3.5.6, but most examples should also work with different minor versions.

Including D3.js

There are multiple ways to include D3.js to your project:

- Using the package manager called bower (recommended), fetch the library by running the **bower install d3#3.5.6** command from the terminal. Then, link the minified CSS file from the **bower_components/** directory in the head section of the web page:

  `<link rel="stylesheet" href="bower_components/d3/d3.min.css">`.

- Using a CDN, such as cdnjs (this requires an active Internet connection while developing), include the minified CSS file from the CDN in the head section of the web page:

  `<link rel="stylesheet" href="https://cdnjs.cloudflare.com/ajax/libs/d3/3.5.6/d3.min.js">`.

- Manually download the 3.5.6 release from GitHub (`https://github.com/mbostock/d3/releases`) and unzip it into the **libs/** directory. Then, link the minified CSS file from the **libs/** directory in the head section of the web page `<link rel="stylesheet" href="libs/d3/d3.min.css">`.

I strongly recommend using the package manager called bower to manage your frontend dependencies. However, in the examples of the book, we will link D3.js directly from cdnjs for simplicity reasons; therefore, all the examples in the source of the book require an active Internet connection.

Finding additional resources

The ultimate resource for D3.js is the WIKI page of the GitHub project, which can be found at `https://github.com/mbostock/d3/wiki`. Here, you will also find examples and a detailed description of the API.

Another great resource for examples is Mike Bostock's page at `http://bl.ocks.org/mbostock` and his blog at `http://bost.ocks.org/mike/`.

For more detailed information and examples, I recommend reading the *Mastering D3.js* book by *Pablo Navarro Castillo*.

Summary

In this chapter, we saw a brief introduction to Responsive Design, Media Queries, and Viewport settings. You learned about relative units and the mobile first design approach for responsive applications.

Later, we introduced Bootstrap and implemented a simple grid system ourselves. This helped us to understand how the responsive fluid grid in Bootstrap works. We saw built-in responsive utilities as well as Media Queries in LESS.

In the last section of this book, we discussed the difference between Pixel and Vector Graphics by comparing the advantages of Canvas, WebGL, and SVG for Responsive Design. We realized that SVG suits very well to implementing responsive visualizations. In the end, we saw a brief introduction to D3.js.

In the next chapter, we will get started with D3.js and implement a simple graphic using data joins, dynamic properties, and simple transformations.

Downloading the example code

You can download the example code files for this book from your account at http://www.packtpub.com. If you purchased this book elsewhere, you can visit http://www.packtpub.com/support and register to have the files e-mailed directly to you.

You can download the code files by following these steps:

Log in or register to our website using your e-mail address and password.

Hover the mouse pointer on the **SUPPORT** tab at the top.

Click on **Code Downloads & Errata**.

Enter the name of the book in the **Search** box.

Select the book for which you're looking to download the code files.

Choose from the drop-down menu where you purchased this book from.

Click on **Code Download**.

Once the file is downloaded, please make sure that you unzip or extract the folder using the latest version of:

WinRAR / 7-Zip for Windows

Zipeg / iZip / UnRarX for Mac

7-Zip / PeaZip for Linux

2
Creating a Bar Chart Using D3.js and SVG

In this chapter, you will learn how to create a bar chart, including proper axis and scales — this requires some basic knowledge in D3, which will also be covered here. You will learn the following:

- How to select and transform DOM elements using D3
- How to use D3 with SVG elements
- How to use a data-driven approach to create visualizations
- How to use data binding and data joins
- How to use dynamic properties
- How to draw lines, areas, and arcs
- How to use scales
- How to draw axis
- How to create a bar chart

First, we will start with some simple DOM selections and transformations of HTML elements and continue creating SVG elements using D3. We will also see how to bind data to the DOM and apply data-driven transformations using data joins and dynamic properties.

In the second section, we will see one of the built-in SVG abstractions in D3 — the so-called generator functions — especially line, area, and arc generators. These abstractions facilitate working with shapes enormously compared to modifying the d attribute of SVG path elements manually.

In the next section, you will learn how to create an axis with axis generators. We will have to scale data points in our dataset along the axis; thus, we will also look into scales. You will learn about linear scales, ordinal scales for non-numeric data, and time scales for time series data.

In the last section, we will apply all the gathered knowledge and create a simple bar chart containing bars (of course), axis, scales, and labels.

Getting started with D3.js

In this chapter, we will create our first bar chart using D3.js and SVG; however, to get there, we will have to go through some basics. These basic concepts are very important because they will give you the freedom to create visualizations for almost everything that you have in your mind. The more of them you know and understand, the more crazy things you can do with D3.

D3.js is a powerful JavaScript library for data-driven DOM manipulations and includes predefined abstractions, transformations, and helpers to work with SVG elements. This makes it an excellent library to write interactive data visualization components using web standards and the complete capabilities of modern web browsers.

Don't worry if you think that this definition is full of fancy buzzwords because in this section, we will walk through all of them. You will understand exactly what they mean and why this makes D3 and SVG a great combination to create visualizations.

Selecting and manipulating DOM elements

D3 lets us select, append, insert, and remove elements in the DOM tree. These functions will look very familiar if you've already worked with other JavaScript frameworks, such as jQuery.

Let's look at some examples to see how this works in D3. We define a simple shopping list in HTML that contains a few items that we need to buy:

```
<ul>
<li>Ham</li>
<li>Cheese</li>
<li>Butter</li>
<li>Bread</li>
</ul>
```

To select elements in the DOM tree, D3 provides the d3.select(selector) and d3.selectAll(selector) methods, which return a **Selection** object. The Selection of the first function contains an array with only a single element, whereas the second one contains an array with multiple elements; both the functions take a CSS3 selector string as an argument (for example, #id, .class, tagname, :pseudo, and more.).

> More information about Selections can be found on the D3 Github page at https://github.com/mbostock/d3/wiki/Selections. More information about CSS3 Selectors can be found on MDN at https://developer.mozilla.org/en-US/docs/Web/Guide/CSS/Getting_started/Selectors.

Under the hood, D3 uses the native document.querySelector(selector) and document.querySelectorAll(selector) functions:

> More information about these functions can be found on MDN at https://developer.mozilla.org/en/docs/Web/API/Document/querySelector and https://developer.mozilla.org/en/docs/Web/API/Document/querySelectorAll.

```
var $ul = d3.select('ul');
var $li = d3.selectAll('li');
```

In the preceding code, we create the $ul Selection of the ul element and the $li Selection, which contains all the li elements.

> Throughout this book, we will use this convention to prefix selections with the $ sign; this will make it easier for you to recognize selections.

Once we have a Selection, we can add more elements to the DOM. One possibility is to append a new DOM node at the end of the Selection using the selection.append (tagName) method; we need to specify the type of element that we want to append by its tag name (for example, div, p, span, li, ul, and more):

```
var $el1 = $ul.append('li');
$el1.text('Milk');
```

In the preceding code, we can see that the `selection.append (tagName)` method returns a Selection that contains the element that was just created. We then use the `selection.text (content)` method to set the inner text of the node to 'Milk'. We can also insert an element before a certain position using the `selection.insert(tagName, selector)` method:

```
var $el2 = $ul.insert('li', ':last-child');
$el2.text('Beer');
```

In the preceding code, we inserted a `li` element with the `Eggs` text before the last child of the list Selection called `$ul`. If we want to remove an element from the DOM, we can call the `selection.remove()` method:

```
$ul.select(':first-child').remove();
```

We remove the first child of the list by calling the `selection.remove()` function. However, we observe that we can call the function directly on the returned object of the `selection.select()` method rather than creating a new variable that contains this element. This technique is called **function chaining** and is often used when working with D3. We can also chain the `selection.insert()` and `selection.append()` functions from the previous examples and apply the `selection.text()` method directly on the returned selection.

We may just want to strike through the last element instead of removing it. The `selection.attr(name, value)` function allows us to modify any attribute of the selected elements:

```
$ul.select(':first-child')
   .attr('class', 'strike-through');
```

In the preceding code, we used the `selection.attr(name, value)` method to access the `class` attribute and set it to `strike-through`. If we now define a class style in the header, we see that the first element has a line through the text

```
<style>
   .strike-through {
      text-decoration: line-through;
   }
</style>
```

Optionally, we can also use the `selection.classed(className, hasClass)` method to add or remove classes to the selections:

```
$ul.select(':first-child')
   .classed('strike-through', true);
```

In the preceding code, we observe that we now only mention a single class that comes handy when you want to toggle a class and keep the others untouched.

 Under the hood, D3 uses the native element.setAttribute(name, value) and element.setAttributeNS(namespace, name, value) functions to access HTML and SVG attributes. This makes D3 very powerful as it directly uses the underlying web standards rather than implementing an abstraction on top.

Manipulating SVG elements

Until now, we have only used D3 to manipulate HTML nodes; if you compare this functionality to jQuery, you learned nothing new or fancy. The good news is that we can also apply all the D3 functions to SVG elements as these elements are also just embedded in the DOM tree.

Let's create a small SVG scene that will contain our elements; we can also add some styling to the svg element for better visibility:

```
<style>
  svg {
    border: 1px dashed black;
    background-color: #efefef;
  }
</style>
<svg width="800" height="400"></svg>
```

Now, we can again use the selection.append() and selection.attr() functions to add elements to the scene and define their attributes. Similar to the previous example, we will also chain the functions together rather than creating a variable for the new element:

```
// Select the SVG element
var $svg = d3.select('svg');

// Append a new circle element
$svg.append('circle')
  .attr({
    cx: 75,
    cy: 75,
    r: 50,
    fill: 'red'
  });
```

In the preceding example, we can select and manipulate SVG elements exactly as we did before with HTML elements. We also observe that the `selection.attr()` function accepts an object that contains multiple `name: value` pairs. This becomes very handy when working with SVG elements as we often have to define multiple attributes at once. The following figure shows the output of this example in the browser:

Simple SVG scene with one circle

Data-driven transformations

In the previous section we saw that the out-of-the box handling of SVG elements makes D3 much more suitable for creating visualizations than for example jQuery. But this is not the only difference between both the frameworks. One of the most important, and also most unique, features of D3 is **data joining**. Data joins are a core concept of D3, and for most of the people this is the most difficult thing to understand while learning D3. However, it is just an extension of **data binding** that also takes the current selection into account. You will quickly find out that it is a very logical rather than mysterious feature.

Data Binding and Dynamic Properties

D3 stands for data-driven documents; but what is a data-driven approach? Data-driven means that the visualization is implicitly defined through the data itself rather than explicitly looping through the data.

Let's take an example using the explicit loop to draw multiple circles on the scene. We are use the same SVG scene as the previous example:

```
// Explicit for loop
for (var i=0;i<5;i++){
  $svg.append('circle')
    .attr({
      cx: 125 * (i + 1),
      cy: 75,
      r: 50,
      fill: 'red'
    });
}
```

In the preceding example, we use an explicit loop to iterate over five numbers to draw five items. The following figure shows the output of the preceding example in the web browser:

Simple SVG scene with multiple elements

Obviously, if we are dealing with datasets, which could be an example extracted from the logs of an application, we don't want to use the `for()` loop but iterate over the data array directly using the `forEach()` loop. Let's create a pseudo data array containing the integers in a `[0, 5)` range (0 is included, but 5 is not included anymore) with the `d3.range(stop)` function:

```
// Create a pseudo dataset
var data = d3.range(5);
```

```
// Explicit forEach loop
data.forEach(function(d, i){
  $svg.append('circle')
    .attr({
      cx: 125 * (d + 1),
      cy: 75,
      r: 50,
      fill: 'red'
    });
});
```

The preceding code already looks a little bit cleaner than the primitive `for()` loop. We observe that the callback function has two attributes—d and i. In general, d is a reference to the current element of the array, and i is the index of the current element in the array. Great! Let's add one final step to transform the loop to a data-driven implementation:

```
// Create a pseudo dataset
var data = d3.range(5);

// Data-driven approach
$svg.selectAll('circle')
.data(data)
  .enter()
  .append('circle')
  .attr({
      cy: 75,
      r: 50,
      fill: 'red'
    })
.attr('cx', function(d, i) { return 125 * (d + 1) });
```

First, I want to draw your attention to the `.data(data)` method; this function is used to bind the `data` array to the Selection. We will discuss this function and the preceding `.enter()` function in more detail in the following section. The second line that I would like to point out is `.attr('cx', function(d, i){ … });` this is the so-called dynamic property—a property that will be dynamically computed by the bound data array where the d and i arguments are used exactly like in the previous `forEach` callback.

Let's summarize the data-driven approach. We bind a data array to a selection of DOM elements and use dynamic properties to define the attributes of the elements by the bound data. Thus, we don't need to loop through the dataset anymore. However, the previous example is a little bit more complicated than just this, which is due to data joins.

Data Join – next-level data binding

As we saw in the previous example, the `selection.data(data)` function binds a dataset to a selection—at least this is what we covered so far. To be more precise, the function does a little bit more than this; it creates a join between a selection and dataset. In the following figure we can see how the data join looks:

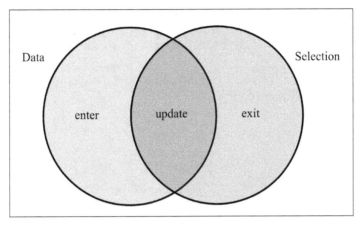

Data join

We can think of the data join by simply comparing the dataset (the red circle in the previous figure) with the Selection (the blue circle in the previous figure) of DOM elements. After comparing the elements of the dataset with the elements in the Selection, we obtain three possible sets of elements:

- The `enter` set: These elements exist in the dataset but not in the Selection, so we want to create them

- The `update` set: These elements exist in the dataset and in the Selection, so we want to update them

- The `exit` set: These elements exist in the Selection but not in the dataset, so we want to remove them

To better understand how this works, we will illustrate it with some code. We will again use the same HTML setup as we did in the previous examples. First, we create a dataset and join it with a Selection:

```
// Create a dataset
var data = d3.range(3);

// Create a data join
var $$circles = $svg.selectAll('circle')
  .data(data);
```

In the preceding example, we first create a dataset in the [0, 3) range. Then, we create a Selection of all the `circle` elements and join them with the dataset. In this case, there are no `circle` elements in the scene, so the Selection is empty. This means that the enter set will contain all the three dataset elements; the update and exit sets will be empty.

> Throughout this book, we will use the convention to the *data joins* prefix with two $ signs; this will make it easier for you to spot a Join and differentiate it from a Selection.

We can now use the `join.enter()` function to return the elements of the enter set (the data array) and add them to the DOM:

```
// Get the enter set
$$circles.enter()
  .append('circle')
  .attr({cy: 75, r: 50})
  .attr('cx', function(d, i) { return 125 * (d + 1) });
```

Calling the `join.enter()` function removes the elements from the enter set and adds them to the update set. Imagine that the enter set is an array, that stores all values from the dataset that are not in the current selection. After calling `.enter()`, one would usually like to add the elements to the DOM. This is why D3 automatically assumes this and moves all the values from the enter set to the update set. Now, after calling `.enter()`, the enter set gets empty and the update set contains all the values from the enter set. We can retrieve the update set using the data join as a Selection:

```
// Modify the update set
$$circles.attr('fill', 'blue');
```

The preceding code will color all the circles in blue because all the elements from the dataset exist now in the Selection of HTML elements.

Finally, we will remove one element from the dataset and join the data again with the Selection; we can then access the exit set by calling the `join.exit()` function and therefore remove the element from the Selection:

```
// Remove an element from the dataset
data.splice(0, 1);

// Create a data join
```

```
$$circles = $svg.selectAll('circle')
  .data(data);

// Get the exit set
$$circles.exit()
  .remove();
```

In the preceding code, we see that we can simply join the dataset again with the Selection to obtain the updated sets. This is very powerful because we can use one function to define how the elements should be drawn on the screen. To update the elements, we will again call the function with the updated dataset; all we need to do is define what happens with the new, existing, and removed elements.

To summarize the data join section, I will list the three functions that we used to access the three sets of the data join:

- The `enter` set: `selection.data(data).enter()`
- The `update` set: `selection.data(data)`
- The `exit` set: `selection.data(data).exit()`

The following figure visualizes the first two steps. We start with an empty selection at the left of the figure; there are no circles yet in the scene. Then, we join the dataset to this empty selection; we obtain an enter set with three elements. For each element in the enter set, we create a circle in the scene and configure its position using the dynamic property for the `cx` attribute.

If we want to update the circles now, we can simply use the data join as a selection. This will return an update set that contains all the three circles.

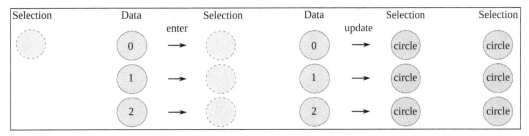

Data join: enter and update sets

In the following figure, we remove one element form the dataset, see what happens in the update, and exit set. After the previous operation, our selection contained three circle elements. If we remove the last element from the dataset, the update set will contain only two elements. The last element of the Selection will now be in the exit set, and it can be removed from the selection in the following step:

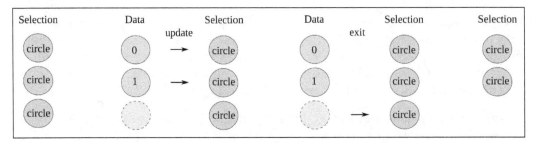

Data join: update and exit set

Using the update pattern

It is a little bit difficult to understand which set to use in order to update specific elements. Therefore, we can use the so-called **Update Pattern** that defines the order in which the elements can be updated.

Let's create a function to illustrate this pattern:

```
function draw(data) {

  // Create a data join
  var $$circles = $svg.selectAll('circle')
    .data(data);

  // Only previously existing elements
  $$circles.attr('fill', 'blue');

  // Only new elements
  $$circles.enter()
    .append('circle');

  // All elements
  $$circles.attr('fill', 'red');

  // Only removed elements
  $$circles.exit()
    .remove();
}
```

If we execute the preceding function multiple times with different data arguments, we can properly define what happens to the following elements:

- Only old (previously existing) elements
- Only new elements
- All elements
- Only removed elements

 There are three great examples about the update pattern on Mike Bostock's Bl.ocks page. I recommend taking a look at all three and trying to understand what exactly is going on in the examples:

- `http://bl.ocks.org/mbostock/3808218`
- `http://bl.ocks.org/mbostock/3808221`
- `http://bl.ocks.org/mbostock/3808234`

Defining an Identifier for the elements

If we look at the API documentation of the `selection.data(data, keyFn)` method, we can see that this function takes a second argument called `keyFn`. With this `keyFn` argument, one can define an `accessor` function that identifies the element of the array in a data join.

Let's look at an example where we use the `draw(data)` function that we implemented in the previous section:

```
// Create 4 elements
draw([0, 1, 2, 3]);
// Update 4 elements
draw([1, 2, 3, 4]);
```

If we don't define a `keyFn` argument, D3 uses the index of the data array as an identifier for the element. In the preceding example, the function first creates four circles; in the second step, it updates these four circles. However, if we look closely, we see that a part of the data is the same but only shifted to the left. Thus, we would rather want a behavior in which 0 gets removed from the Selection, [1, 2, 3] stays the same, and 4 gets added to the Selection. We can achieve this using the array value as an identifier rather than the array index. Let's define a custom `keyFn` that returns the array element as identifier.

```
var $$circles = $svg.selectAll('circle')
  .data(data, function(d, i){ return d; });
```

In the preceding example, we define an identifier function in the same way as the callback functions that we used in dynamic properties.

Drawing shapes with D3

D3 is a great library to create web visualizations because it includes a lot of useful abstractions when working with SVG elements. In this section, we will look at some of these SVG abstractions to draw shapes. These abstractions for drawing shapes are called generators in D3; we will mainly use the line-, area-, and arc-generators when creating visualizations.

 All SVG shape abstractions can be found in the D3 Github page at `https://github.com/mbostock/d3/wiki/ API-Reference#d3svg-svg`.

Drawing Lines and Curves

If you've ever used the SVG `path` element and the `d` attribute to create custom shapes or Bézier curves, you already know that this is not as easy as it should be. Those who have never used the SVG `path` element only need to know that you would have to learn a special syntax to define and concatenate control points for a Bézier curve.

 You can find more information about the `d` attribute on MDN at `https://developer.mozilla.org/en-US/docs/Web/ SVG/Attribute/d`.

Thankfully, D3 provides a great abstraction to draw lines. Let's take a look at a simple example. First, let's create a dataset containing the x and y coordinates of some points:

```
var data = [
  [100, 100], [200, 350], [300, 50],
  [400, 200], [500, 250], [600, 40], [700, 100]
];
```

Now, we want to create a line generator that returns the first element of a data point as the x coordinate and the second value of the data point as the y coordinate:

```
var line = d3.svg.line()
  .x(function(d, i) { return d[0]; })
  .y(function(d, i) { return d[1]; });
```

Perfect! This is already our line generator. The advantage is that we only have to define the structure of the line generator, that is, where in the dataset it can find the x and y coordinates, and we can then draw any dataset that follows the same structure. Let's draw the line; we need to use the `selection.datum()` method to bind one specific datum to the selection. In contrary to the previously discussed data joins, this function will not compute a join but only returns a selection. Then, we can apply the line generator to the d attribute of the path, which will implicitly look for the bound data and creates the proper d string:

```
$svg.datum(data)
  .append("path")
  .attr("d", line);
```

The following figure shows a result of this example in the web browser:

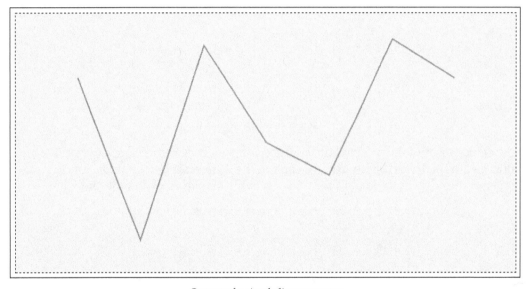

Output of a simple line generator

In the previous example, you learned how to create a simple line generator that only connects the points of the dataset together. We can now easily define an interpolation method on the line generator in order to draw a smooth line:

```
var line = d3.svg.line()
  .x(function(d, i) { return d[0]; })
  .y(function(d, i) { return d[1]; })
  .interpolate('cardinal');
```

In the preceding example, we used the `cardinal` interpolation, which is a similar interpolation technique used in Bézier curves. If we look at the resulting line in the following figure, we see that the lines between the data points are now interpolated:

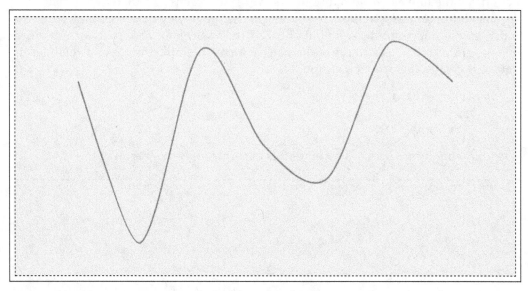

Output of an interpolated line

The smoothness of the interpolation can be controlled by the `.tension(value)` function. In the following figure, we can see the difference between tension `1`, which is the edgy inner line, to tension `0.5`, which is the smooth outer line:

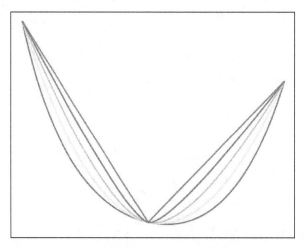

Line with different tension values

Drawing Areas between curves

Similar to the line generator, D3 also provides an area generator that allows us to use 2 y coordinates: y0 and y1. Let's first create a dataset where the first element of the data point contains the x value, the second element the first y coordinate, and the third element the second y coordinate:

```
var data = [
  [100, 100, 100], [200, 350, 200], [300, 50, 50],
  [400, 200, 350], [500, 250, 375], [600, 40, 100], [700, 100, 100]
];
```

Now, we can create an area generator similar to the previous example:

```
var area = d3.svg.area()
  .x(function(d, i) { return d[0]; })
  .y0(function(d, i) { return d[1]; })
  .y1(function(d, i) { return d[2]; })
  .interpolate('cardinal');
```

Finally, we apply the area generator to the d attribute of the path element:

```
$svg.datum(data)
  .append("path")
  .attr("d", area);
```

The following figure shows the result of the created area path:

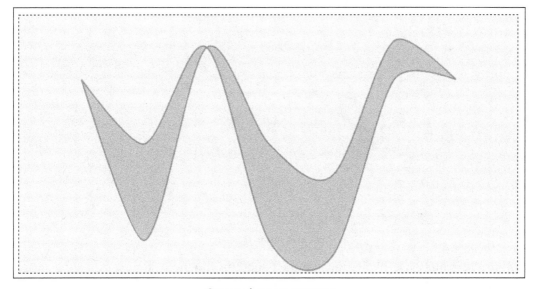

Output of an area generator

Drawing arcs

The third complex shape that is often used in visualizations is an arc. D3 also provides a generator function for this to easily draw arcs with polar coordinates. Again, if you have ever dealt with arcs in SVG, you will probably be very glad to know this generator.

Let's create an arc generator:

```
var arc = d3.svg.arc()
   .innerRadius(40)
   .outerRadius(100)
   .startAngle(0)
   .endAngle(Math.PI);
```

In the preceding code, we see that we can define inner and outer radius as well as the start and ending angles of the arc in radiant. Similarly to the previous example, we can now generate the d attribute for a `path` element:

```
$svg.append("path")
   .attr("d", arc)
   .attr("transform", "translate(200, 200)");
```

In the previous example, we observe that we need to translate the arc a little bit in order to make it visible. The output of the example in the web browser is displayed in the following figure:

Output of an arc generator

D3 provides more useful methods on the generator functions, for example, the `arc.centroid()` method. This function returns the center of the arc shape and suits perfectly to display labels with an arc.

Creating Scales and Axis

D3 is often mistaken for a charting library, which is not really correct. D3 provides loads of built-in functions to easily create interactive charts; however, it is not a charting library. One of these typical built-in charting helpers are the closely related *Scales* and *axis generators*. You will learn about them in this section.

At the end of this section, we want to be able to draw a simple axis as the one in the following figure. Therefore, we need to scale our dataset to a specific pixel range (using Scales) and create all the SVG elements for the axis (using axis generators):

Axis in D3

Mapping data values to a Pixel Range with scales

The concept of scales is very important when we deal with graphics and visualization. It is a common task to scale values from a certain domain to a certain range of pixels. We need them to create tick values on axes, and we need them to scale our data points to the area of the chart.

The following figure explains the problem a little bit better. Imagine we want to map a certain domain of values in our dataset (let's say only the positive values) to a certain pixel range in the chart (let's say from 20px to 460px). Scales give us exactly this functionality in D3:

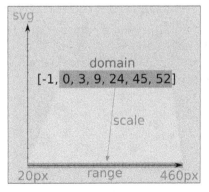

Scale in D3

I want to emphasize again on the naming convention in D3. We are speaking in terms of domains about a certain extent of the dataset and in terms of ranges about a certain pixel range. Whenever we want to apply linear transformations (as in the previous figure), we speak about *linear* scales.

Linear Scales for linear Mappings

Let's take a look at the simplest mappings-linear transformations, and create one according to the previous figure:

```
var scale = d3.scale.linear()
    .domain([0, 52])
    .range([20, 460]);
```

In the preceding code, we observe that we can use the d3.scale.linear() function to create an identity scale (maps domain [0, 1] to a range [0, 1]), and then specify a domain and a range for this scale.

Let's see how this scale object works; actually, we can just call it as a function, and it will now scale any value from the dataset to the pixel range. Let's try this and map the whole dataset with this scale:

```
console.log([0, 3, 9, 24, 45, 52].map(scale));
```

If we check the output in the Developer Tools console, we get an array similar to the following:

```
[20, 45.38461538461539, 96.15384615384615, 223.0769230769231,
400.7692307692308, 460]
```

We can see in the output of the preceding function that every value from the input array is transformed with the scale function to the new pixel range.

Ordinal scale for Mapping non-numeric data

Often, we have to deal with non-numerical — the so-called ordinal data; if we look into a bar chart, we usually have values that belong to a certain label rather than a specific x value. In this case, it's perfect to use ordinal scales in order to map these non-numeric values to the pixel range.

First, let's create a simple one:

```
var data = ['Bread', 'Eggs', 'Milk', 'Beer'];

var scale = d3.scale.ordinal()
    .domain(data)
    .range([0, 1, 2, 3]);
```

In the preceding example, we first create a dataset, which we also define as the domain of the ordinal scale. In the second step, we define a range on which the data values should be projected. If we map the whole dataset, the result is equal to our defined range:

```
console.log(data.map(scale));
// [0, 1, 2, 3]
```

If we want to define a continuous pixel range for the discrete points, we can use the `.rangePoints()` method instead. Let's look at an example:

```
var scale = d3.scale.ordinal()
  .domain(data)
  .rangePoints([0, 10]);

console.log(data.map(scale));
// [0, 3.3333333333333335, 6.666666666666667, 10]
```

In addition, we can also define a range that considers the structure of a bar chart—namely the `.rangeBands()` method. This function takes into account the fact that we need to shift the bars half the width of one bar to the left to match the tick values.

```
var scale = d3.scale.ordinal()
  .domain(data)
  .rangeBands([0, 10]);

console.log(data.map(scale));
// [0, 2.5, 5, 7.5]
```

Time scales for Mapping time series data

Finally, there also exists a scale, when working with time series data, which maps JavaScript Date objects to pixel ranges. Let's see an example; first, we define an array of Date objects:

```
var data = [
  new Date(2015, 8, 1),
  new Date(2015, 8, 2),
  new Date(2015, 8, 3),
  new Date(2015, 8, 4)
];
```

Now, we can define our scale; we will use the `d3.extent(data)` function to return the `[min, max]` value of the data:

```
var scale = d3.time.scale()
  .domain(d3.extent(data))
  .range([20, 460]);
```

If we map our dataset to the new range, we get values inside the `[20, 460]` range:

```
console.log(data.map(scale));
// [20, 166.66666666666666, 313.3333333333333, 460]
```

Creating Axis

When creating axis in D3, we want to use the feature provided by scales in order to map the dataset to a range of pixels. In the following figure, we can see an example from the Developer Tools and how the final result of the axes looks:

D3 axis selected in the Developer Tools

First, we need to define a scale for the axis that handles the mapping:

```
var scale = d3.scale.linear()
  .domain([0, 10])
  .range([20, 380]);
```

Now, we can create an axis generator that works very similarly to the previously mentioned generators:

```
var axis = d3.svg.axis()
  .scale(scale);
```

Finally, we can draw the axis by simply passing the generator function to the `.call()` method on any (empty) selection in which we want to create the axis:

```
d3.select('svg')
  .call(axis);
```

That was it, no magic, no struggle.

 D3 has loads of built-in functionality when dealing with axes. It's absolutely worth taking a look at the corresponding section in the Wiki page available at `https://github.com/mbostock/d3/wiki/SVG-Axes`.

A simple bar chart

Congratulations, you've gathered all the knowledge to build your first bar chart; and this is exactly what we will do in this section. In the following figure, we will create a bar chart that has axis, scales, bars, and labels.

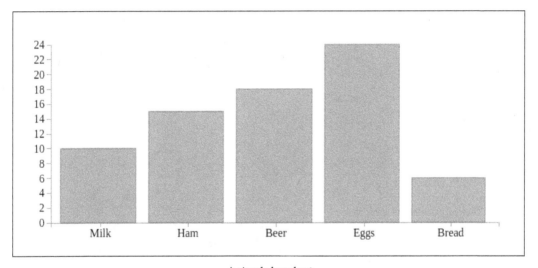

A simple bar chart

Let's start with a simple setup—a blank HTML page that loads the D3 library from the bower components directory. In addition, we define the `crispEdges` rendering for path elements in the header:

```
<!doctype HTML>
<html>
<head>
<title>Bar Chart</title>
<script src="bower_components/d3/d3.min.js"></script>

<style>
        .axis path, .axis line {
          fill: none;
```

```
      stroke: #999;
      shape-rendering: crispEdges;
    }
    .data rect {
      stroke: red;
      fill: rgba(255, 0, 0, 0.5);
    }
</style>

</head>
<body>
<script>
    // Our code goes here
</script>
</body>
</html>
```

Now, we can start to write JavaScript inside the `script` element and initialize the chart dimensions and the data:

```
// Define the dimensions
var width = 800;
var height= 400;

// Define the inner margins
var pad = 75;

// Define the data
var data = [
  {y: 10, label: 'Milk'},
  {y: 15, label: 'Ham'},
  {y: 18, label: 'Beer'},
  {y: 24, label: 'Eggs'},
  {y: 6, label: 'Bread'}
];
```

As a next step, we can already create the `svg` element and set its dimensions properly:

```
var $svg = d3.select('body')
  .append('svg')
  .attr({
    width: width,
    height: height
  });
```

Identical to the previous examples, the $svg variable again references the Selection with the svg root element. Let's create a container for the data and axes:

```
var $axesGroup = $svg.append('g').attr('class', 'axis');
var $dataGroup = $svg.append('g').attr('class', 'data');
```

Now, we look back at our dataset and define an accessor function for the x values called xKey and the y values called yKey. These functions will become useful when we need to access these values in the dataset:

```
var xKey = function(d){ return d.label; };
var yKey = function(d){ return d.y; };
```

With these two functions, we can easily map the dataset to an array of only x or y values by simply calling data.map(xKey) or data.map(yKey). Let's create a scale for the x axis. This scale maps labels (ordinal values) to the horizontal pixel range of the chart:

```
var xScale = d3.scale.ordinal()
    .domain(data.map(xKey))
    .rangeRoundBands([pad, width - pad], 0.1);
```

In the preceding code, we use the x values of the dataset as a domain and project them on the non-overlapping bands using the .rangeRoundBands() method to the range called [pad, width - pad]. Now, we can continue creating a scale for the y axis; this will be a simple linear scale:

```
var yScale = d3.scale.linear()
    .domain([0, d3.max(data, yKey)])
    .range([height - pad, pad]);
```

This scale was a little bit easier than the previous ordinal scale; we simply map the domain of [0, max] where max is the greatest y value in the dataset. Then, we project it to a pixel range of [height - pad, pad]. One might wonder why we changed the order of the range values for the y scale. This is due to the orientation of the coordinate system in SVG where 0 along the y coordinate is at the top, whereas, in our chart, a 0 value should be mapped at the bottom.

Let's continue and create the axis generators; we need one for the x axis and one for the y axis. In the x axis, we can already define the number of ticks by specifying it in the .ticks() method. It should be equal to the number of elements in the dataset. The y axis should be oriented vertically with the tick values on the left-hand side. We can specify this with the .orient() method:

```
var xAxis = d3.svg.axis()
    .scale(xScale)
```

```
    .ticks(data.length);

var yAxis = d3.svg.axis()
  .scale(yScale)
  .orient('left');
```

After creating the axis generators, we can already draw the axis. We can do this by simply passing the axis generator to the `.call()` method on a Selection of an empty container. We also need to shift the axis to the proper position in the chart. The x axis should be at the bottom and the y axis at the left:

```
$axesGroup.append('g')
  .attr('class', 'x axis')
  .attr('transform', 'translate(0, ' + (height - pad) + ')')
  .call(xAxis);

$axesGroup.append('g')
  .attr('class', 'y axis')
  .attr('transform', 'translate(' + pad + ')')
  .call(yAxis);
```

Let's look at the output of the preceding code in the browser; we will be able to see the axes:

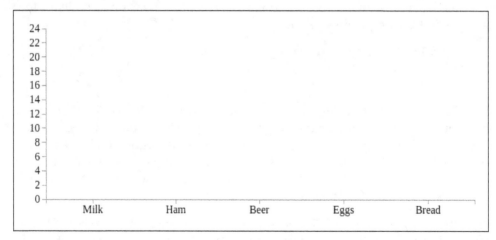

Axes of the chart

The previous figure shows that everything looks good so far. Great, we are almost there. Finally, we can start drawing the bars in our chart. Before we start drawing bars, we need to define the width of our bars as the maximal width divided by the number of bars:

```
var barWidth = (width - 2*pad) / (data.length + 1);
```

Now, we can create a data join for the bars using the x value of the dataset as the identifier:

```
var $$bars = $dataGroup.selectAll('rect')
  .data(data, xKey);
```

We can go ahead and create the `rect` node for all elements in the enter set:

```
$$bars.enter()
  .append('rect');
```

Next, we move the rectangles to their proper position in the chart by simply using the scale function on the values of the dataset:

```
$$bars
  .attr('x', function(d) { return xScale(d.label); })
  .attr('y', function(d) { return yScale(d.y); })
  .attr('height', function(d) { return yScale(0) - yScale(d.y); })
  .attr('width', barWidth);
```

Please note that, due to the SVG coordinate system, we need to define the y values and height of the bars by drawing them from the top to the bottom. Finally, for completeness, we also add the last step of our data join and remove all the elements from the exit set:

```
$$bars.exit()
  .remove();
```

In this example, we will never remove bars from the chart, but it is good practice to include the preceding lines to your code. This will become very useful once you put the code in a function and call it multiple times.

Let's make a slight adjustment to the chart to better stick to the responsive visualization topic. As a general rule, one can say that every time we define static pixel values, the result will look bad on some or the other device. So, what can we change? Well, never use explicit static pixel values but relative values extracted from the parent element.

If we follow this strategy, we can use the width of the body element for our chart width. All other values (the height and padding) can be defined relative to the width of the chart:

```
var $body = d3.select('body');

// Define the dimensions
var width = $body[0][0].clientWidth;
var height = width * 0.5;

// Define the padding
var pad = width * 0.1;
```

If we replace the old dimensions with these new computed dimensions, the chart will look good on every device that opens the web page. Great! I am very happy about how far you have come in this chapter; you can be very proud of yourself. You build your first (almost) responsive bar chart!

Summary

In this chapter, you learned how to select DOM elements and do data-driven transformations using data joins and dynamic properties. We also saw how to use shape and axis generator functions to quickly create common shapes such as lines or areas.

In the end of this chapter, we built our first simple (almost) responsive bar chart. The bar chart already adapts to the width of the browser window on the page load, but it doesn't get recomputed when we change the browser dimensions.

In the next chapter, we will take a look at loading, filtering, and grouping data. This is very important because almost always we will have to load remote data in a certain format (such as CSV) and then process, filter, or group it afterwards in order to visualize it.

3
Loading, Filtering, and Grouping Data

In the previous chapter, you learned to draw a simple bar chart. In this chapter, you will learn to load, parse, and display real data from a remote location with this chart. In this chapter, you will learn the following:

- Why we need to preprocess our data
- How to filter outliers
- How to map data to another representation
- How to aggregate information
- How to load data using D3
- How to parse strings using Regular Expressions
- How to parse date strings
- How to format numbers
- How to group flat data

First, we will start with some basic preprocessing steps that are always necessary. We will use the `filter` function to filter outliers and unexpected values from the dataset; we will also use the map function to access inner properties of array elements.

Then, you will learn about reduce functions and how they can help in aggregating and extracting information out of the data. We will implement our own simple reduce function and also take a look at the ones provided within D3.

Next, you will learn how to load data from remote locations. Spoiler alert, this will be very easy with D3. However, we need to make sure that the loaded data can be understood by JavaScript, and therefore, we sometimes need to parse the files. You will learn to use Regular Expressions to split strings into chunks, which can be accessed as arrays via JavaScript.

We will then take a look at parsing and formatting date, time and numeric values. This is very important because, when we deal with dates in text files, they are always represented as strings rather than JavaScript objects.

In the last section, you will learn about grouping flat data structures, such as CSV, that contain hierarchical information to nested JavaScript objects. Together, with the previous section, we will be able to extract any information that we want out of a dataset and plot it in a chart.

Preprocessing data

In this chapter, you will learn about preprocessing and that it is an important step when you deal with real-world data. If we want to design a robust visualization that can handle different remote data sources, we need to make sure we process the data beforehand. Datasets can have outliers, can be noisy, can have different representations, can have nested objects, can be flat, and so on. You can see that this list is very long.

Thus, whenever we deal with real data, we need to process it before using it in a visualization; this step is called preprocessing.

Filtering data to remove outliers

As a first preprocessing step, we will look at filters. Filters are array operators that return an array containing a subset of the original elements. In the following figure, we see an example of such an operation:

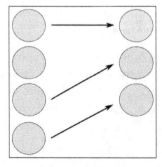

Filtering a dataset

Let's try an example. We load the following array from a remote
data source:

```
var data = [
  {x: 1, y: 6},
  {x: 2, y: undefined},
  {x: 3, y: 4},
  {x: 4, y: 2},
  {x: undefined, y: 3},
  {x: 5, y: 3},
  {x: 6, y: 7},
];
```

We see that the preceding dataset contains some values that are undefined.
Whenever we work with real data, we should expect that some data values are not
defined or properly formatted. If we want to remove these values from our array,
we can use the `array.filter(filterFn)` operator. The `filter` function called
`filterFn` will be evaluated for each element in the dataset and needs to return either
`true` or `false`. Here, `false` means that the element will not appear in the returned
array. Let's write a filter function that returns only valid objects:

```
var filtered = data.filter(function(d, i){
  if (d.x !== undefined && d.y !== undefined) {
    return true;
  }
  return false;
});
```

In the previous code, we see a typical `filter` function, which returns `true` if
`d.x` and `d.y` are defined and `false` otherwise. However, we can write this more
elegantly and simply return the `if` expression:

```
var filtered = data.filter(function(d, i){
  return d.x !== undefined && d.y !== undefined;
});
```

> Be careful with implicit type coercions when dealing with
> numerical values. If you write `d.x && d.y` instead, you
> will implicitly cast the numbers to Boolean values. And
> guess what kind of Boolean you'll get when you cast a
> numerical `0`. Well, you get `false`.

This looks much shorter and cleaner, great! Now, we can also create a filter that only returns the data points that have a y value greater than a certain number, as we can see in the following example:

```
var filtered = data.filter(function(d, i){
  return d.y > 5;
});
```

Mapping data to access inner properties

It happens very often that the values that you want to visualize are somehow nested and hidden inside the array objects. You can easily access this data by mapping the whole array to a different array representation. This mapping operation is visualized in the following figure:

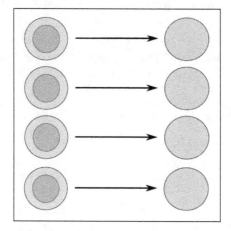

Mapping of one dataset to a different representation

Let's take a look at an example dataset where we would like to extract the number of counts from the data points:

```
var data = [
  {x: 1, inner: {count: 5}},
  {x: 2, inner: {count: 4}},
  {x: 3, inner: {count: 1}},
  {x: 4, inner: {count: 8}},
  {x: 5, inner: {count: 3}},
  {x: 6, inner: {count: 5}}
];
```

We see in the preceding dataset that the information is nested in the `count` property of the `inner` object. We can use the `array.map(mapFn)` method with a mapping function called `mapFn` to return elements for each element of the new array representation:

```
var mapped = data.map(function(d, i){
  return {
    x: d.x, y: d.inner.count
  }
});
```

The `mapped` array now contains objects with the x and y properties that you can use to generate our visualizations, as you learned in the previous chapter. Although, this looks very trivial, many people have problems applying the map function properly.

Aggregate data to extract valuable information

Another important preprocessing step in data visualization is aggregating values of the dataset. The general idea is that of a `reduce` function. In the following figure, we can see the schematics of a reduce function; it is an array operation that returns one single value for multiple elements.

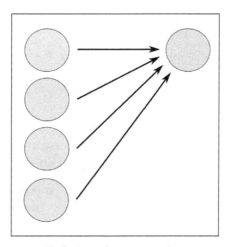

Reducing a dataset to a value

You don't have to be a `MapReduce` expert to use this function; most likely, you are already using many of these functions already today. Just think about a function that returns the sum of all the elements in an array or a function that returns the minimal or maximal value of an array — these are all reduce functions.

Reduce functions help us to aggregate values that we want to visualize. Let's take a look at a simple example where we would like to display the number of counts from an inner object:

```
var data = [
  {x: 1, inner: [5, 1, 1]},
  {x: 2, inner: [2, 1, 1]},
  {x: 3, inner: [5, 3, 2]},
  {x: 4, inner: [3, 5, 4]},
  {x: 5, inner: [4, 1, 2]},
  {x: 6, inner: [5, 3, 1]}
];
```

In the preceding dataset, we want to aggregate the values of the inner property in order to visualize them; we want to use the sum of the aggregation. We can now combine a map operation and `array.reduce(reduceFn, startValue)` to transform the dataset to a nice representation. The reduction `reduceFn` is a function that takes four arguments; `previous`, `current`, `arr` and `index`, and it returns a value for the next element. We can also assign a `startValue` to represent the `previous` attribute of the first element in the array. Let's take a look at a very simple reduction function, a simple sum:

```
function sum(a, b){
  return a + b;
}
```

Now, we can use the `reduce` function to sum up all the values in the `inner` property:

```
var reduced = data.map(function(d, i){
  return {
    x: d.x, y: d.inner.reduce(sum, 0)
  }
});
```

Again, the resulting array consists of objects with the x and y properties, whereas the y property now contains a sum of all the inner values.

We can also nest the map and reduce operations in order to aggregate some more nested data. Let's take a look at an example of a nested dataset:

```
var data = [
    {x: 1, inner: [{count: 5}, {count: 1}, {count: 1}, ...]},
    {x: 2, inner: [{count: 2}, {count: 1}, {count: 1}, ...]},
    {x: 3, inner: [{count: 5}, {count: 3}, {count: 2}, ...]},
    {x: 4, inner: [{count: 3}, {count: 5}, {count: 4}, ...]},
    {x: 5, inner: [{count: 4}, {count: 1}, {count: 2}, ...]},
    {x: 6, inner: [{count: 5}, {count: 3}, {count: 1}, ...]}
  ];
```

Now, we need to map the `inner` values to an array which can then be used by the reduce function:

```
var reduced = data.map(function(d, i){
  return {
    x: d.x, y: d.inner
      .map(function(d){
        return d.count;
      }).reduce(sum, 0)
  }
});
```

In the preceding code, we first use a map returning the elements of the count property; then we apply the reduce function on the returned array. You can already see that by nesting the preprocessing functions, we can aggregate and extract a lot of data from the dataset.

Reduce functions in D3.js

As you might already wonder, D3 comes with a lot of handy reduce functions which can be applied to arrays. However, using the d3 functions, you always have to pass the array as an argument. In all d3 reduce functions, you can use the `accessor` function, which is passed to a map operation before the reduce operation is done. This works exactly as in the previous example.

We can extract the extrema of a dataset with any of the following:

- `d3.min(arr, accessor)`,
- `d3.max(arr, accessor)`
- `d3.extent(arr, accessor)`

Let's take an example of the last one:

```
var data = [
  {x: 1, inner: {count: 5}},
  {x: 2, inner: {count: 4}},
  {x: 3, inner: {count: 1}},
  {x: 4, inner: {count: 8}},
  {x: 5, inner: {count: 3}},
  {x: 6, inner: {count: 5}}
];

var extent = d3.extent(data, function(d, i){
  return d.x;
});
```

The `extent` function in the preceding code returns the array called `[min, max]` with the minimal and maximal x value of the dataset.

To extract other statistical information from the dataset, we can use the following:

- `d3.mean(arr, accessor)`,
- `d3.median(arr, accessor)`,
- `d3.variance(arr, accessor)`
- `d3.deviation(arr, accessor)`

> The `filter`, `map`, and `reduce` functions have their origin in functional programming as they work on an input array, transform it independently of a state or context, and output a new array at the end. A benefit of using a reduce function over a simple loop is that you execute your code inside a local scope, whereas in a loop you would be still in the same scope and maintain a state.
>
> Talking about performances, the `filter`, `map`, and `reduce` functions are rarely faster than the alternative with a custom loop. This mainly depends on the JavaScript engine and how it optimizes these functions. However, as I said before, they allow the developer to write more beautiful and cleaner code, as they work in a separated scope independently of a state. If this interests you, you should definitely check out more about Functional Programming!

Loading and parsing remote data

In this section, we want to visualize real data rather as in sample dataset; hence, we need to understand how to load data from remote locations. In JavaScript, you can use the native **XMLHttpRequest (XHR)** object to fetch data within your application. D3 implements not only a wrapper for the native XHR call, but it also implements wrappers for loading different data types and parsing them automatically.

Here is a list of some high-level wrappers in D3:

- `d3.text(url[, mimeType][, callback])`: This loads a plain text file with a `mimeType` from an URL; the data is handed over as a string to the `callback` where the parsing must be done manually
- `d3.json(url[, callback])`: This loads and parses a JSON file from an URL; the data is passed as an object in the `callback`
- `d3.xml(url[, mimeType][, callback])`: Loads and parses an XML file from an URL, the data is passed as an object in the `callback`

- `d3.html(url[, callback])`: This loads and parses an HTML file from an URL; the data is passed as an object in the `callback`

- `d3.csv(url[, accessor][, callback])`: This loads and parses a CSV (comma-separated) file from an URL; the data is passed as an object in the `callback` and can be automatically mapped with an `accessor` function

- `d3.tsv(url[, accessor][, callback])`: This loads and parses a TSV (tabulation-separated) file from an URL; the data is passed as an object in the `callback` and can be automatically mapped with an `accessor` function

The `callback` function is called when all data is loaded; the data will be provided as an argument to the `callback` function.

> If we try to load data from the local machine, we will most likely get a **Cross Origin Request** error. This is a security policy of modern browsers that prevents the loading of local data into the browser. However, we can use a static fileserver, such as the node package called `http-server` or the python command called `python -m SimpleHTTPServer 8000`.
>
> If you don't want to span up a web server to prevent this security issue, you can also disable this in the browser settings or while startup:
>
> - In Firefox, enter `about:config` in the address bar and set `security.fileuri.strict_origin_policy` to false
> - In Chrome and Chromium, close all open instances and start a new session called `chrome.exe—allow-file-access-from-files` or `chromium-browser --allow-file-access-from-files`

We can see that, with the built-in data loading functions, it's very easy to load remote data with D3. Let's take a look at an example; we will load a CSV file:

```
// data source: Mike Bostock
var url = 'https://gist.githubusercontent.com/mbostock/32.../data.
csv';

d3.csv(url, function(data){
  draw(data);
});
```

In the preceding code, we use a `draw` function that contains the code for the bar chart that we developed in the previous chapter. You can also look at the source code of all code examples to see the full function.

The CSV file contains a few lines similar to the following code:

```
key,value,date
Group1,37,04/23/12
Group2,12,04/23/12
Group3,46,04/23/12
Group1,32,04/24/12
Group2,19,04/24/12
```

If we run the previous code, the resulting chart looks like the following figure:

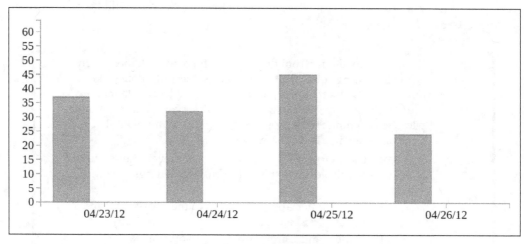

Bar chart with remote data

In the preceding chart, we see quite some errors that happen when we simply try to plot a dataset as it is. There exist multiple data points per day — one for each group — but we are only plotting one. This is an amazing example, why, even in very small and trivial datasets we need some kind of preprocessing for the data.

Let's, for example, filter out only the data for the key called `Group1`. To do so, we only have to use a small filter function on the data:

```
d3.csv(url, function(data){
  draw(data.filter(function(d){
    return d.key === 'Group1';
  }));
});
```

In the preceding example, we use a filter that returns `true` if the `key` property matches `'Group1'`. In the following figure, we can see the result of the example:

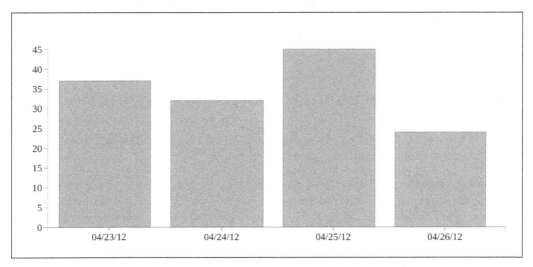

Plotting data from Group 1

This already looks very interesting and much better than the previous example. However, we are only plotting the data from the first group. We will learn how to aggregate the data from all groups in the last sections of this chapter.

Another interesting observation from the previous figure is that we simply plot the raw date values as we read them from the remote location. We use them as strings, which makes them very uncomfortable to work with. Here is where parsing date values comes in quite handy.

Parsing any string data

Data visualizations often display data from multiple sources; therefore, we cannot guarantee that the datasets will always be in a CSV, TSV, or even JSON format. To load and parse raw data, for example, unformatted log data, we can use the `d3.text` function and parse the dataset on our own.

Let's look at a typical access log entry from a web server. It contains timestamps and user agents of the visitors of a website:

```
66.249.64.129 - - [22/Nov/2014:01:56:01 +0100] "GET / HTTP/1.1" 302
487 "-" "Mozilla/5.0 (compatible; Googlebot/2.1; +http://www.google.
com/bot.html)"
```

There are some questions that come into one's mind if he/she wants to plot the preceding data. How should one aggregate the data? Do we want to sum all visitors per minute, per hour, or per day, or do we just want to sum the visitors by browser or by country of origin? Once we've parsed the data into a readable format, we can easily do all of the preceding things (you will learn this in the last section of the chapter). However, we first need to parse the string into a format that JavaScript can use.

Splitting strings using Regular Expressions

The first step in processing a string is always splitting it into smaller chunks of words. If the log entries have been created by a program, they usually have some kind of structure but very often a very strange one.

If we take a closer look at the entries in the log file, we can see that single log entries are separated by a newline character called \n. Well, we actually don't see the character, but we can see the line breaks only at the end of the complete log entry.

We also observe that the - and " characters are some sort of separators between the logical parts of the entry. To split the string properly, we always have to find these separators. Now, we can use Regular Expressions and the `string.split(expr)` function to split the string into an array of smaller chunks. In the following figure, we can see this operation visualized:

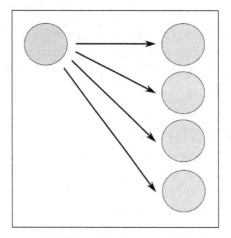

Split a string into an array

Let's see this in action and split the log file into an array of log entries:

```
var lines = data.split(/\n/g);
```

Now, we can use the map function to access the inner elements of the line array and split them into logical chunks:

```
var lines = data.split(/\n/g)
  .map(function(line){
    return line.split(/[-"]/g);
  });
```

In the preceding code, we use the two Regular Expressions called /\n/g and /[-"]/ g. In the first one, we simply look for matches of the \n character, and in the second one, we look for either the - or " character. In both cases, we use the greedy flag to search the whole string rather than stopping at the first occurrence.

> More information about Regular Expressions in JavaScript can be found on MDN at https://developer. mozilla.org/en/docs/Web/JavaScript/ Reference/Global_Objects/RegExp.
>
> Usually, it is very tricky to get Regular Expressions to work properly. I recommend using a tool such as https:// regex101.com/ to evaluate your expression before you throw them into your code.

The following figure visualizes how we are processing the string. The first split happens from the blue to the red layer. Then, we use map to split all of the elements from the red to the green layer. This all happens in the previous four lines of the code:

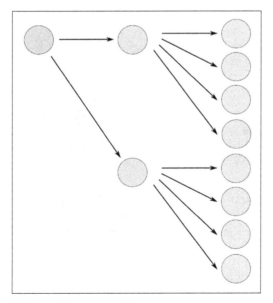

Splitting nested strings into arrays

You can already see that by nesting multiple split functions, you can split the string into an array of substrings that contain your information. In the next step, we need to parse date time values from different string representation into the JavaScript representation.

Parsing dates from strings

As we saw already in the example of the log data, we will often have to deal with time series data in a specific string format. To transform, compare, and display Dates properly throughout the visualization, we have to first parse the string to a valid JavaScript `Date` object. Fortunately, D3 includes a powerful `datetime` parser to convert `datetime` strings into `Date` objects and vice versa.

To create such a formatter, we have to use the `d3.time.format()` function, which returns a formatter. We can then either use the formatter as a function to format Date objects or use the `.parse()` method to parse the `datetime` strings. Let's take a look at an example:

```
// Create a formatter
var formatter = d3.time.format('%Y-%m-%d');
// Parse a string to a Date object
formatter.parse("2015-01-01");
// Thu Jan 01 2015 00:00:00 GMT+0100 (CET)
```

As we've already discussed, we can also use the `formatter` function to convert `Date` objects into strings in order to style and format them:

```
// Create a formatter
var formatter = d3.time.format('%Y-%m-%d');
// Format a Date object to a string
formatter(new Date(2015, 0, 1));
// "2015-01-01"
```

 To make yourself familiar with the native Date object, you can take a look at the Mozilla Developer website at `https://developer.mozilla.org/de/docs/Web/JavaScript/Reference/Global_Objects/Date`.

As we can observe in the preceding code example, D3 uses formatter specifiers to define the format of the `datetime` string. Here, you can find a list of specifiers that can be used to for declaring the `datetime` format, which I took from my previous book *Data Visualization with D3 and AngularJS* by *Packt Publishing*:

- `%a`: Abbreviated weekday name
- `%A`: Full weekday name

- `%b`: Abbreviated month name
- `%B`: Full month name
- `%c`: Date time format `%a %b %e %H:%M:%S %Y`
- `%d`: Zero-padded day of month `[01, 31]`
- `%e`: Space-padded day of month `[ 1, 31]`
- `%H`: Hour in 24-hour format `[00, 23]`
- `%h`: Hour in 12-hour format `[01, 12]`
- `%j`: Zero-padded day of the year `[001, 366]`
- `%m`: Zero-padded month `[01, 12]`
- `%M`: Zero-padded minute `[00, 59]`
- `%L`: Zero-padded milliseconds `[000, 999]`
- `%p`: AM or PM
- `%S`: Zero-padded second `[00, 61]`
- `%U`: Zero-padded week number of the year (Sunday as first day of the week) `[00, 53]`
- `%w`: Weekday (starting with Sunday) `[0, 6]`
- `%W`: Zero-padded week number of the year (Monday as first day of the week) `[00, 53]`
- `%x`: Date format `%m/%d/%Y`
- `%X`: Time format `%H:%M:%S`
- `%y`: Zero-padded year without century `[00, 99]`
- `%Y`: Year with century
- `%Z`: Time zone offset (for example `-0700`)
- `%a`: Abbreviated weekday name
- `%a`: Abbreviated weekday name
- `%%`: The literal character `%`

 You can find more information about `datetime` specifiers on the D3 Github page at `https://github.com/mbostock/d3/wiki/Time-Formatting`.

Parsing and formatting numeric values

We will not only have to deal with date and time strings but also with numeric values. In the case of integer and float values, we can use native functions to parse strings and D3 number formatters for formatting and styling them.

Integers and floats can be parsed easily by the `parseInt()` and `parseFloat()` functions. However, sometimes it is convenient to use the short + notation to cast strings to numeric values.

```
// Parsing strings to numbers
var i = parseInt("5.0", 10);
var f = parseFloat("3.8");

// Short notation
var s = "932.2";
var j = +s;
```

In the preceding code, we see that it's very convenient to use the native functions and the short + notation for converting strings into numbers. We also observe that, most of the time, we will use the basis 10 in the `parseInt` function.

Formatting number values into strings in D3 is very similar to formatting date values into strings. However, D3 can only format numbers into strings; for string to number conversion, you can use the native functions that we just discussed. Again, we need to first create a formatter using the `d3.format(specifier)` function; then, we can use the `formatter` as a function to format numbers. Let's take a look at an example:

```
// Create a formatter
var formatter = d3.format('.2f');

// Format a number object to a string
formatter(3.12e-1);
// "0.31"
```

The specifier argument again defines the structure of the formatted string values that we want to generate. This can be composed in the following form:

```
[fill]align] [sign] [symbol] [0] [width] [,] [.precision] [type]
```

Each of these options allows you to customize different properties of the generated string. Here, I just want to provide a list of all possible type specifiers, which is also taken from my previous book *Data Visualization with D3 and AngularJS* by *Packt Publishing*:

- e: exponent
- g: general
- f: fixed
- d: Integer
- r: Rounded to precision if specified
- %: Percentage
- p: Percentage rounded to precision if specified
- b: Binary
- o: Octal
- x: Hexadecimal
- X: Hexadecimal with upper case letters
- c: Unicode character
- s: SI-suffixed and rounded

Let's take a look at some selected examples using different type specifiers:

```
console.log(d3.format('e')(0.3123));      // "3.123e-1"
console.log(d3.format('g')(31.223e3));    // "31223"
console.log(d3.format('f')(31.23));       // "31"
console.log(d3.format('d')(124));         // "124"
console.log(d3.format('%')(0.23));        // "23%"
console.log(d3.format('p')(0.2314));      // "23.14%"
console.log(d3.format('b')(23));          // "10111"
console.log(d3.format('s')(31.223e3));    // "31.223k"
```

 You can find more information about number specifiers on the D3 Github page at https://github.com/mbostock/d3/wiki/Formatting.

Grouping data

Most of the time when we find data resources on the Internet, it has a flat data structure just as a comma separated list. But often, it contains hierarchical structured data. In D3, it is very easy to group data together by creating nested tree structures of the dataset. To achieve this, we can use the d3.nest() operator. This operator creates a nest object, which can further define a grouping key via the .key() method and a sorting function via the .sortKey() method. These functions can also be repeated to create multiple nested layers of the flat data structures. Let's take a look at the dataset:

```
var values = [
  {
    date: "04/23/12",
    key: "Group1",
    value: "37"
  },
  {
    date: "04/23/12",
    key: "Group2",
    value: "12"
  },
  {
    date: "04/23/12",
    key: "Group3",
    value: "46"
  }, ...
];
```

First, we create a nest function that will then group our data accordingly:

```
var nest = d3.nest()
  .key(function(d, i){
    return d.date;
  });
```

A nest now implements an .entries(data) method, which can takes dataset as input and returns a grouped result of the flat data structure. If you are curious, you can take a look at the output of the preceding nest function applied to our dataset.

```
console.log(nest.entries(data));
```

The previous code shows a result such as the following figure in the developer tools of the browser:

```
                                 B05166_01_Group_Data.html:33
▼ [Object, Object, Object, Object]
  ▼ 0: Object
      key: "04/23/12"
    ▼ values: Array[3]
      ▼ 0: Object
          date: "04/23/12"
          key: "Group1"
          value: "37"
        ►   proto  : Object
      ▼ 1: Object
          date: "04/23/12"
          key: "Group2"
          value: "12"
        ►   proto  : Object
      ▼ 2: Object
          date: "04/23/12"
          key: "Group3"
          value: "46"
        ►   proto  : Object
        length: 3
      ►   proto  : Array[0]
    ►   proto  : Object
  ▼ 1: Object
      key: "04/24/12"
    ► values: Array[3]
    ►   proto  : Object
  ► 2: Object
  ► 3: Object
    length: 4
  ►   proto  : Array[0]
```

Nest function applied to dataset

 You can find more information about nests on the D3 Github page at `https://github.com/mbostock/d3/wiki/Arrays#d3_nest`.

As a logical next step, we can now apply map and reduce functions to count objects, occurrences, and values and map them into a simpler structure. It would be a good exercise to map the preceding hierarchical object into an array containing {x, y} elements with y being the sum of all values for each object.

Let's use this nest function together with the reduce function to draw a chart similar to the previous example. However, we want to group the entries per day and sum over all groups now.

We can continue doing so by mapping the `value` property of the elements in the `values` array and suming the values up. We use the `+string` short notation to convert the `value` properties into numeric values:

```
draw(nest.entries(data).map(function(d){
  return {
    date: d.key,
    value: d.values.map(function(d){
      return +d.value;
    })
    .reduce(sum, 0)
  }
}));
```

In the preceding code, we first apply the nest function on the original dataset. Then, we use a map function to apply the next processing step to every group of the nested groups. In the inner processing step, we map the array of values to an array of numbers and sum it up via the reduce function. We can write this a bit more elegantly using the `d3.sum(arr, accessor)` method, which combines the map and reduce steps. The resulting code is here:

```
draw(nest.entries(data).map(function(d){
  return {
    date: d.key,
    value: d3.sum(d.values, function(d){
      return +d.value;
    })
  }
}));
```

Great, this looks much cleaner and is also super readable. Now, we can see the result of the browser in the following figure:

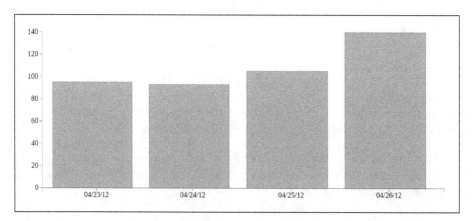

Grouped and aggregated values

Summary

In this chapter, you learned about data preprocessing in order to make it displayable for the visualization. We saw how to filter unexpected data, how to map data to a different representation, and how to aggregate data.

We took a look at loading data from remote resources and custom-parsing via Regular Expressions. We saw how to split a string into an array of elements that can then be used for further processing. In the end, you learned how to use D3 for grouping flat data into nested objects. This helped us to ultimately extract all the desired information out of the remote dataset.

In the next chapter, we will take the previously generated chart and make it responsive. You will learn what it exactly it means for a chart to be responsive and how we can use Bootstrap to achieve this.

4
Making the Chart Responsive Using Bootstrap and Media Queries

In the previous chapter, you learned all about loading, parsing, filtering, and grouping data from real sources. This gives us everything we need to design responsive charts using Bootstrap and Media Queries on some real data. In this chapter, you will learn the following:

- Learning absolute and relative units in the browsers
- Understanding what a responsive chart really is
- Drawing charts with percentage values
- Scaling charts using the `viewBox` and `preserveAspectRatio` attributes
- Adapting charts using JavaScript event listeners
- Learning to adapt the resolution of the data
- Using Bootstrap's Media Queries
- Understanding how to use media queries in CSS, LESS, and JavaScript
- Learning the usage of Bootstrap's grid system

First, we will discuss the most important absolute and relative units that are available in modern browsers. You will learn the difference between absolute pixels, relative percentages, `em`, `rem`, and many more.

In the next chapter, we will take a look at what it really needs for a chart to be responsive. Adapting the width to the parent element is one of these requirements, and you will learn three different ways to implement this. After this section, you will know when to use percentage values, viewport scaling, or event listeners. We will also take a look at adapting the data resolution—another important property of responsive charts.

In the next section, we will explore Media Queries and how we can use them to make viewport depended responsive charts. We will take the advantage of Bootstrap's definitions of Media Queries for the most common device resolutions to integrate them into our responsive chart using CSS or LESS. Finally, we will also see how to include Media Queries into JavaScript.

In the last section of this book, we will look at Bootstrap's grid system and understand how to integrate it seamlessly with the charts. This will give us not only great flexibility but also makes it easier to combine multiple charts to one big dashboard application.

Units and lengths in the browser

Creating a Responsive Design, website, or graphics strongly depends on the units and lengths that a browser can interpret. We can easily create an element that fills the whole width of a container using the percentage values that are relative to the parent container, whereas achieving the same result with absolute values can be very tricky. Thus, mastering responsive graphics also means knowing all the absolute and relative units that are available in the browser.

Units for absolute lengths

The most convenient and popular way in web designing and development is to define and measure lengths and dimensions in absolute units, usually in pixels. The reason for this is that designers and developers often want to specify the exact dimensions of an object. The pixel unit called px has been introduced as a visual unit based on a physical measurement to read from a device in the distance of approximately one arm's length; however, all modern browsers can also allow the definitions of lengths based on physical units. The following list shows the most common absolute units and their relation to each other:

- cm: centimeters (*1 cm = 96 px/2.54*)
- mm: millimeters (*1mm = 1/10th of 1 cm*)
- in: inches (*1 in = 2.54 cm = 96 px*)
- pt: points (*1 pt = 1/72th of 1 in*)
- px: pixels (*1 px = 1/96th of 1 in*)

More information about the origin and meaning of the pixel unit can be found in the CSS3 specification at `http://www.w3.org/TR/css3-values/#viewport-relative-lengths`.

Units for relative lengths

In addition to absolute lengths, relative lengths are expressed as the percentage of the width or height of the parent element. It has also been a common technique to style the dynamic elements of web pages. Traditionally, the `%` unit has always been the unit of choice for the preceding reason. However, with CSS3, a couple of additional relative units have found their way into the browsers to define the length relative to the font size of the element.

Here is a list of some relative length units that have been specified in the CSS3 specifications and soon will be available in modern browsers:

- `%`: The percentage of the width/height of absolute container
- `em`: This is the factor of the font size of the element
- `rem`: This is the factor of the font size of the root element
- `vw`: 1% of viewport's width
- `vh`: 1% viewport's height
- `vmin`: 1% of viewport's smaller dimension (either `vw` or `vh`)
- `vmax`: 1% of viewport's larger dimension (either `vw` or `vh`)

I am aware, that as web developers, we cannot really take the advantage of a technology that will be supported soon; however, I want to point out one unit that will play an important role for web developers in the future: the `rem` unit. The `rem` unit defines the length of an element based on the font size of the root node (the `html` node in this case) rather than the font size of the current element such as `em`.

This `rem` unit is very powerful if we use it to define the length and spacing of a layout because the layout can also adapt when the user increases the font size of the browser (for example, for readability). I want to mention that Bootstrap 4 will replace all the absolute pixel units for the Media Queries with the `em and rem` units mostly because of this exact reason.

If we look at the following figure, we also see that the `rem` units are already supported in all major browsers. I recommend you to start replacing all your absolute pixel units of your layout and spacing by `rem` units:

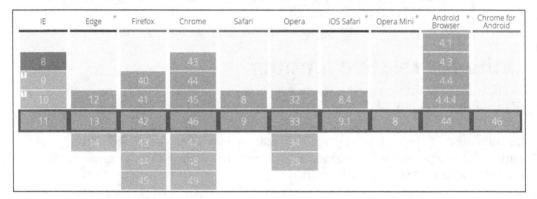

IE	Edge *	Firefox	Chrome	Safari	Opera	iOS Safari *	Opera Mini *	Android * Browser	Chrome for Android
								4.1	
8			43					4.3	
9		40	44					4.4	
10	12	41	45	8	32	8.4		4.4.4	
11	13	42	46	9	33	9.1	8	44	46
	14	43	47		34				
		44	48		35				
		45	49						

The cross-browser compatibility of the rem units (source: http://caniuse.com/#feat=rem)

However, percentage units are not dead; we can still use them when they are appropriate. We will use them later to draw SVG elements with dimensions based on their parent elements' dimensions.

Units for resolution

To round up the section of relative and absolute units, I want to mention that we can also use resolutions in different units. These resolution units can be used in Media Queries together with the `min-resolution` or `max-resolution` attribute:

- `dpi`: dots per inch
- `dpcm`: dots per centimeter
- `dppx`: dots per px unit

Mathematical expressions

We often have the problem of dealing with rational numbers or expressions in CSS; just imagine defining a three-column grid with a width of 33% per column or the need for computing a simple expression in the CSS file. CSS3 provides a simple solution for this.

`calc(exp)` computes the mathematical expression called `exp`, which can consist of lengths, values, and the operators called +, -, /, and *.

Note that the + and - operators must be surrounded by whitespace. Otherwise, they will be interpreted as a sign of the second number rather than the operator. Both the other operators * and / don't require a whitespace, but I encourage you to add them for consistency.

We can use these expression in the following snippets:

```
.col-4 {
  width: calc(100% / 3);
}
.col-sp-2 {
  width: calc(50% - 2em);
}
```

The preceding examples look great; however, as we can see in the following figure, we need to be aware of the limitations of browser compatibility:

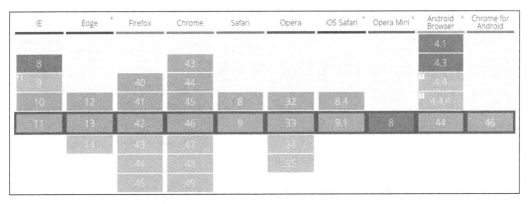

The cross-browser compatibility of the calc() expression (source: http://caniuse.com/#feat=calc)

Responsive charts

Now that we know some basics about absolute and relative units, we can start to define, design, and implement responsive charts. A responsive chart is a chart that automatically adapts its look and feel to the resolution of the user's device; thus, responsive charts need to adapt the following properties:

- The dimension (width and height)
- The resolution of data points
- Interactions and interaction areas

Adapting to the dimensions is the most obvious thing. The chart should always scale and adapt to the width of its parent element. In the previous section, you learned about relative and absolute lengths, so one may think that simply using relative values for the chart's dimensions would be enough. However, there are multiple ways with advantages and disadvantages to achieve this; in this section, we will discuss three of them.

Adapting to the resolution of the data is a little less obvious and often a neglected thing. The resolution of data points (the amount of data point per pixel) should adapt so that we can see more points on a device with a higher resolution and less points on a low resolution screen. In this section, we will see that this can only be achieved using JavaScript event listeners and redrawing/updating the whole chart manually.

Adapting interactions and interaction areas is important for not just using different screen resolutions but also different devices. We interact differently with a TV than with a computer, and we use different input devices on a desktop and mobile phone. However, the chart should allow interactions and interaction areas that are appropriate for a given device and screen resolution. You will learn more about responsive interactions in the following chapter.

Using relative lengths in SVG

The first and most obvious solution for adapting the dimensions of a chart to its parent container would be the use of relative values for lengths and coordinates. This means that we define the chart once with relative values, and the browser takes care of recomputing all the values when the dimensions of the parent container changes. There is no manual redrawing of the chart required.

Let's look at the bar chart example of the previous chapters. You can find the complete source code in the code examples of this chapter that are provided with this book.

First, we will add some CSS styles to scale the SVG element to the full width of the parent container:

```
.chart {
  height: 16rem;
  position: relative;
}
.chart > svg {
  width: 100%;
  height: 100%;
}
```

Next, we modify all our scales to work on a range of `[0, 100]` and subtract padding from both sides:

```
var xScale = d3.scale.ordinal()
  .domain(flatData.map(xKey))
  .rangeBands([padding, 100 - 2*padding]);

var yScale = d3.scale.linear()
  .domain([0, d3.max(flatData, yKey)])
  .range([100 - 2*padding, padding]);
```

Finally, we can draw the chart as before, but simply adding percentage signs (`%`) to the end of the attributes to indicate the use of percentage units:

```
$$bars
  .attr('x', function(d) { return (xScale(d.x) + i*barWidth ) + '%';
})
  .attr('y', function(d) { return yScale(d.y) + '%'; })
  .attr('height', function(d) { return (yScale(0) - yScale(d.y)) +
'%'; })
  .attr('width', barWidth + '%')
  .attr('fill', colors(data.key));
```

You can observe, that the code for plotting the bars was only modified slightly. Now it uses percentage values for coordinates and attributes. However, the effect of this small change is enormous. In the following figure, we can see the result of the chart in a browser window:

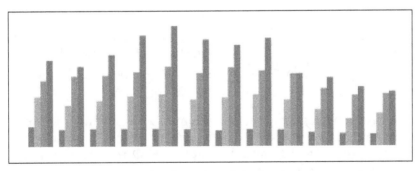

The bar chart using relative lengths

If we increase the size of the browser now, the bar chart scales nicely to the full width of the parent container. We can see the scaled chart in the following figure:

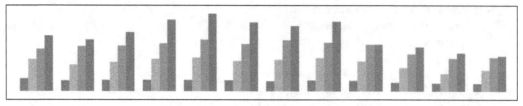

The scaled bar chart using relative lengths

If you are not impressed by it now, you better be. This is awesome in my opinion because it leaves all the hard work of recomputing the SVG element dimensions to the browser. We don't have to care about them, and this native computation gives us maximal performance.

The previous example shows how to use percentage values to create a simple bar chart. However, what isn't explained so far is why we didn't add any axis and labels to the chart. Well, despite the idea that we can exploit native rescaling of the browser, we also need to face the limitations of this technique: relative values are only allowed in standard attributes, such as width, height, x, y, cx, cy but not in SVG paths or transform functions.

Conclusion about using relative lengths

While this sounds as an excellent solution (and indeed it is wonderful for certain use cases), it has two major drawbacks:

- Percentage values are not accepted for SVG transform attributes and the d attribute in path elements but only in standard attributes
- Due to the fact that the browser is recomputing all the values automatically, we cannot adapt the resolution of the data of charts

The first point is the biggest drawback, which means we can only position elements using the standard attributes width, height, x, y, cx, cy, and so on. However, we can still draw a bar chart that seamlessly adapts according to the parent elements without the use of JavaScript event listeners.

The second argument doesn't play a huge role anymore compared to the first one and can be circumvented using additional JavaScript event listeners, but I am sure you get the point.

Scaling the viewport

SVG has some powerful features, such as the `viewBox` and `preserveAspectRatio` attributes that allow automatic rescaling of the whole graphic to the SVG viewport. Using these two attributes, we can draw the chart with absolute values in a defined area, scale this area automatically to the parent container, and define the handling of the aspect ratio of the original dimensions.

Let's start from the beginning. We call the SVG viewport the visible area of the SVG element; usually, we see by default the standard coordinate system. The `viewBox` attribute allows us to scale a certain area of the coordinate system to the dimension of the viewport. We do so by defining the area in the coordinate system by a rectangular through the upper-left and lower-right points.

I will demonstrate it by modifying the bar chart example. First, let's use some absolute dimensions, for example, `400x300`. In our case, we will define this by a fixed width and an aspect ratio factor:

```
var width = 400;
var aspectRatio = 4.0 / 3.0;
var height = width / aspectRatio;
```

We also keep the CSS code from the previous example, which scales the SVG element to the full width of the parent container.

Now, we can draw the complete chart using these absolute dimensions and finally add the `viewBox` attribute to scale the chart to the viewport:

```
var $svg = d3.select(chart).append('svg')
  .attr('viewBox', '0 0 ' + width + ' ' + height)
```

That is all. Now, let's assume we draw the chart in an element with approximately the dimensions that we used to create the chart. We can see the output of such a result in the following figure:

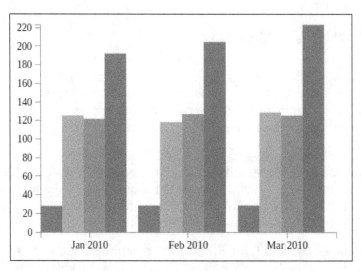

The bar chart is scaled to viewport

We observe that the chart looks pretty nice, and it scales perfectly into the full width, preserving the aspect ratio automatically. But here, we can already guess some of the drawbacks of this solution:

- The aspect ratio is fixed
- The chart should have similar initial coordinates, such as the containing element

The first point should be somehow clear; we define an aspect ratio and this is why the chart keeps the same aspect ratio even when it is redrawn on a different element. The second point, however, is crucial for this implementation. Let's look at the following chart that had initially been created with the 800 x 600 scale:

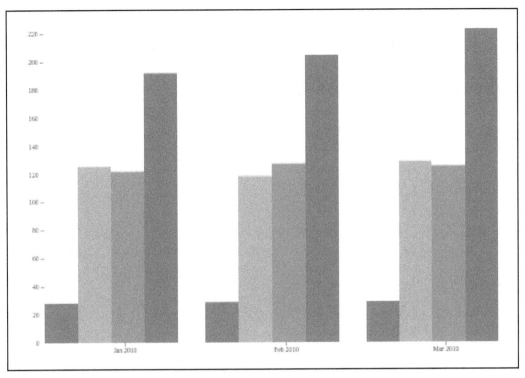

The big chart is scaled to the small viewport

We can see it immediately; the chart is downscaled to fit the dimensions of the container, and therefore, the font and the axis become unreadable because the ticks are too small. The opposite thing happens when we use `800 x 600` as an initial scale. We can see the effect in the following figure where the ticks are now so big that they are overlapping:

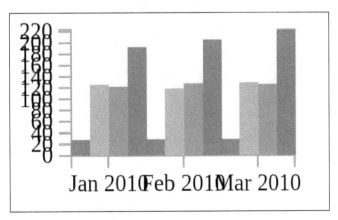

The small chart is scaled to big viewport

We observe in the previous chart that the axis and axis ticks are scaled too much due to the upscaling to the viewport. Once again we note that for this technique, it is necessary to draw the chart on an useful range of coordinates.

Prevent Strokes from Scaling

We can add simple options to prevent strokes from scaling through the transformations caused by the `viewBox` attribute. To do so, we have to add the following CSS snippet to the chart:

```
.chart path, .chart line, .chart text {
  vector-effect: non-scaling-stroke;
}
```

The `vector-effect` property (that only allows the `none`, `inherit`, and `non-scaling-stroke` values) is the attribute that can achieve exactly this. However, I don't really understand why there are no more supported values to, for example, prevent the scaling of fonts, and so on.

The following figure shows a downscaled example of a bar chart where the stroke widths stay untouched:

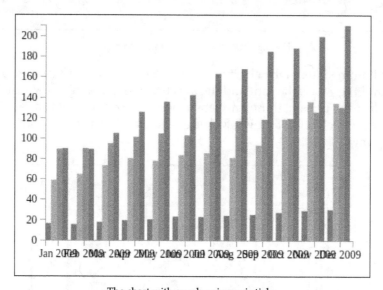

The chart with overlapping axis ticks

Okay, now, let's again look at this example and think about the major drawback — the fixed aspect ratio. Often, the user resizes the web page to see more/less information. Here, for example, axis ticks overlap because either the tick labels are too long or the chart width is too small. However, if we resize the window, the chart will scale up and the output will look similar to the following figure. It is just scaled across both the dimensions and preserving aspect ratio. We observe that there is no way to better arrange the data across the longer x axis in order to enhance the visibility of the chart and avoid the overlapping of labels on the axis:

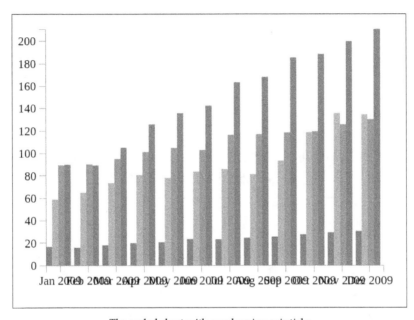

The scaled chart with overlapping axis ticks

We observe that the image simply scales without changing the aspect ratio and the representation of the data. Thus, due to the simple scaling, the tick labels overlap on the bigger chart.

Preserving the Aspect Ratio

If we intend to modify the aspect ratio of the scaled image, we can do so. We can additionally set the preserveAspectRatio attribute to none or some other values to scale the image with other aspect ratios than the xMidYMid default:

```
var $svg = d3.select(chart).append('svg')
  .attr('viewBox', '0 0 ' + width + ' ' + height)
  .attr('preserveAspectRatio', 'none');
```

Using none aspect ratio can, for example, scale the image into the viewport without preserving the aspect ratio as shown in the following figure:

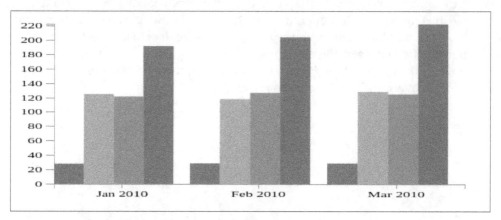

The chart scaled using the preserveAspectRatio none

Per default, browsers use the `xMidYMid` setting to scale the chart to the maximal centered dimension by possibly preserving the aspect ratio of the original chart:

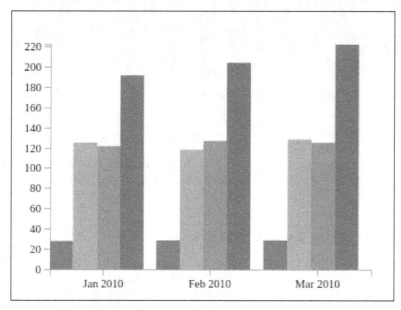

The chart scaled using preserveAspectRatio xMidYMid (default)

The conclusion of using Viewport scaling

While this is an excellent solution for certain use cases, it has two major drawbacks:

- The whole chart always gets scaled; we can only prevent strokes from scaling
- Due to the fact that the browser is recomputing all the values automatically, we cannot adapt the resolution of the data of charts

Also, the first point is the major drawback. Scaling the chart to the viewport is great in certain situations: however, it is not very flexible, especially because we would also be scaling fonts and because we need to preserve the aspect ratio; so, we cannot scale the chart to arbitrary dimensions. Moreover, we have to be extremely careful with using initial dimensions that are not too big or small in order to not scale thin lines too big or scale details too small.

The second argument doesn't play a huge role anymore compared to the first one and can be circumvented using some additional JavaScript event listeners.

Using the JavaScript resize event

The last option is to use JavaScript event handlers and redraw the chart manually when the dimensions of the parent container change. Using this technique, we can always measure the width of the parent container (in absolute units) and use this length to update and redraw the chart accordingly. This gives us great flexibility over the data resolution, and we can also adapt the chart to a different aspect ratio when needed.

The native resize event

Theoretically, this solution sounds brilliant; we simply watch the parent container or the SVG container (if it uses a width of 100%) for `resize` events, and then we redraw the chart when the dimensions of the element change. However, there does not exist a native `resize` event on the `div` or `svg` element; modern browsers only support the `resize` events on the `window` element. Hence, it only triggers if the dimensions of the browser window change. This also means that we need to clean up listeners once we have removed a chart from the page.

Although this is a limitation, in most cases, we can still use the `window resize` event to adapt the chart to its parent container; we have to just keep this in our mind.

Let's always use the parent container's absolute dimensions to draw and redraw the chart; we need to define the following things inside a `redraw` function:

```
var width = chart.clientWidth;
var height = width / aspectRatio;
```

Now, we can add an resize event listener to the window element and call the `redraw` function whenever the window dimensions change:

```
window.addEventListener('resize', function(event){
  redraw();
});
```

The benefit of this solution is that we can do anything we want in the redraw function, for example, modifying the aspect ratio, adapting the labels of the axis, or modifying the number of displayed elements.

The following figure shows a resized version of the previous chart; we observe that this time, the axis ticks adapt nicely and don't overlap anymore. Moreover, the axis ticks now take the full space available:

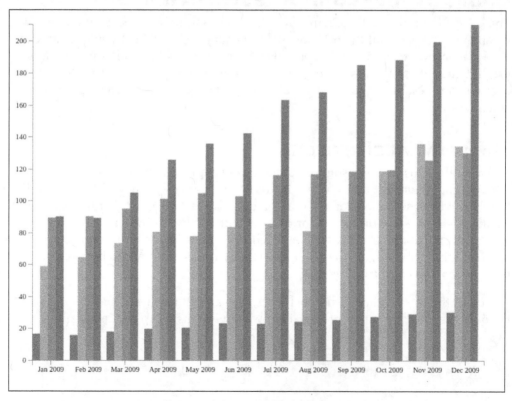

The resized chart with adapted axis ticks

Adapting the resolution of the data

However, there is another problem that can be solved nicely using these types of manual redraws: the problem of data resolution. How much data should be displayed in a small chart and how much in a bigger chart?

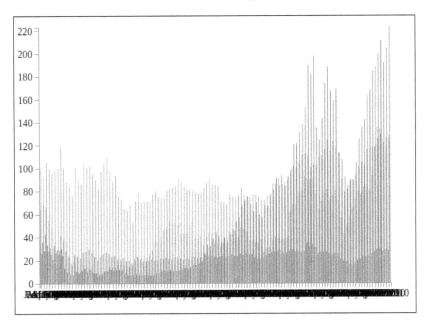

The small chart with high data resolution

I think you agree that in the preceding figure, we display too much data for the size of the graphic. This is bad and makes the chart useless. Moreover, we should really adapt the resolution of the data according to the small viewport in the redrawing process.

Let's implement a function that only ever returns the i-th element of an array:

```
function adaptResolution(data, resolution) {
  resolution = resolution ? Math.ceil(resolution) : 1;
  return data.filter(function(d, i) {
    return i % resolution === 0;
  });
}
```

Great, let's define a width-depended data resolution and filter the data accordingly:

```
var pixelsPerData = 20;
var resolution = pixelsPerData * (flatData.length) / width;
```

In the preceding code, we observe that we can now define the minimum amount of pixel that one data point should have, and we remove the amount of values accordingly by calling the following:

```
var flatDataRes = adaptResolution(flatData, resolution);
```

The following image shows a small chart with a low number of values, which is perfectly readable even though it is very small:

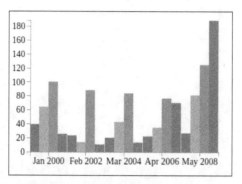

The small chart with a proper data resolution

In the next figure, we can see the same chart based on the same data, drawn with a bigger container. We immediately observe that the data resolution adapts accordingly making the chart look nice:

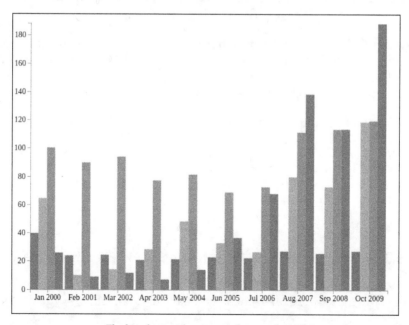

The big chart with a proper data resolution

The conclusion of using resize events

This is the most flexible solution, and therefore, in many situations, it is the solution of choice. However, you need to be aware that there are also certain drawbacks in using this solution:

- There is no easy way to listen for resize events of the parent container
- We need to add event listeners
- We need to make sure that event listeners are removed properly
- We need to manually redraw the chart

Using Bootstrap's Media Queries

As we already discussed in the first chapter, Bootstrap is an awesome library that gets you started quickly with new projects. It includes not just huge amounts of useful HTML components, but also normalized and standardized CSS styles. A particular one is the implementation of Media Queries for four typical device types (five types in Bootstrap 4). In this section, we will take a look at how to make use of these Media Queries in our styles and scripts. A great thing about Bootstrap is that it successfully standardizes the typical device dimensions for web developers; thus, beginners can simply use them without rethinking over and over which pixel width could be the most common one for tablets.

Media Queries in CSS

The quickest way to use Bootstrap's Media Queries is to simply copy them from the compiled source code. The queries look as follows:

```
/* Extra small devices (phones, etc. less than 768px) */
/* No media query since this is the default in Bootstrap */

/* Small devices (tablets, etc.) */
@media (min-width: 768px) { ... }

/* Medium devices (desktops, 992px and up) */
@media (min-width: 992px) { ... }

/* Large devices (large desktops, 1200px and up) */
@media (min-width: 1200px) { ... }
```

We can easily add these queries to our CSS styles and define certain properties and styles for our visualizations, such as four predefined widths, aspect ratios, spacing, and more to adapt the chart's appearance to the device type of the user.

Bootstrap 4 is currently in alpha; however, you can already start using the predefined device types in your CSS. The reason I am strongly arguing for Bootstrap 4 is due to its shift toward the em units instead of pixels:

```
// Extra small devices (portrait phones, etc.)
// No media query since this is the default in Bootstrap

// Small devices (landscape phones, etc.)
@media (min-width: 34em) { ... }

// Medium devices (tablets, etc.)
@media (min-width: 48em) { ... }

// Large devices (desktops, etc.)
@media (min-width: 62em) { ... }

// Extra large devices (large desktops, etc.)
@media (min-width: 75em) { ... }
```

Once again, the huge benefit of this is that the layout can adapt when the user increases the font size of the browser to enhance readability.

Media Queries in LESS/SASS

In Bootstrap 3, you can include Media Query mixins to your LESS file, which then gets compiled to plain CSS.

To use these mixins, you have to create a LESS file instead of CSS and import the Bootstrap variables.less file. In this file, Bootstrap defines all its dimensions, colors, and other variables. Let's create the style.less file and import variables.less:

```
// style.less
@import "bower_components/bootstrap/less/variables.less";
```

Perfect, that's all. Now, we can go ahead and start using Bootstrap's device types in our LESS file:

```
/* Extra small devices (phones, etc. less than 768px) */
/* No media query since this is the default in Bootstrap */

/* Small devices (tablets, etc.) */
@media (min-width: @screen-sm-min) { ... }

/* Medium devices (desktops, etc.) */
```

```
@media (min-width: @screen-md-min) { ... }

/* Large devices (large desktops, etc.) */
@media (min-width: @screen-lg-min) { ... }
```

Finally, we need to use a LESS compiler to transform our `style.less` file to plain CSS. To achieve this, we run the following command from the terminal:

```
lessc styles.less styles.css
```

As we can see, the command requires the LESS compiler called `lessc` being installed. If it's not yet installed on your system, go ahead and install it:

npm install -g less

 If you are new to LESS, I recommend you to read through the LESS documentation on `http://lesscss.org/`. Once you check out LESS, you can also look at the very similar SASS format, which is favored by Bootstrap 4. You can find the SASS documentation at `http://sass-lang.com/`.

We can use the Bootstrap 4 Media Queries in a SASS file by the following mixins:

```
@include media-breakpoint-up(xs) { ... }
@include media-breakpoint-up(sm) { ... }
@include media-breakpoint-up(md) { ... }
@include media-breakpoint-up(lg) { ... }
@include media-breakpoint-up(xl) { ... }
```

In my opinion, including Bootstrap's LESS/SASS mixins to the styles of your visualization is the cleanest solution, because you always compile your CSS from the latest Bootstrap source, and you don't have to copy CSS into your project.

Media Queries in JavaScript

Another great possibility of using Bootstrap's Media Queries to adapt your visualization to the user's device is to use them directly in JavaScript. The native `window.matchMedia(mediaQuery)` function gives you the same control over your JavaScript as Media Queries gives us over CSS.

Here is a little example on how to use it:

```
if (window.matchMedia("(min-width: 1200px)").matches) {
  /* the viewport is at least 1200 pixels wide */
} else {
  /* the viewport is less than 1200 pixels wide */
}
```

In the preceding code, we see that this function is quite easy to use and adds almost infinite customization possibilities to our visualization.

> More information about the `matchMedia` function can be found on the Mozilla website at `https://developer.mozilla.org/de/docs/Web/API/Window/matchMedia`.

However, besides using the `watchMedia` function directly, we can also use a wrapper around the native API call. I can recommend the `enquire.js` library by Nick Williams, which allows you to declare event listeners for viewport changes. It can be installed via the package manager bower by running the following command from the terminal:

```
bower install enquire
```

Then, we need to add `enquire.js` to the website and use:

```
enquire.register("screen and (min-width:1200px)", {

    // triggers when the media query matches.
    match : function() {
      /* the viewport is at least 1200 pixels wide */
    },

    // optional; triggers when the media query transitions
    unmatch : function() {
      /* the viewport is less than 1200 pixels wide */
    },
});
```

In the preceding code, we see that we can now add the `match` and `unmatch` listeners almost in the same way as listening for resize events, it's just much more flexible.

> More information about `enquire.js` can be found on the Github page of the project at `https://github.com/WickyNilliams/enquire.js`.

If we would like to use the Bootstrap device types, we could easily implement them (as needed) with `enquire.js` and trigger events for each device type. However, I prefer being very flexible and using the bare wrapper.

Using Bootstrap's grid system

Another great and quick way to make your charts responsive and play nicely together with Bootstrap is to integrate them into Bootstrap's grid system. The best and cleanest integration, however, is to separate concerns and make the visualization as general and adaptive as possible.

Let's take our bar chart example with the custom resize events and integrate it into a simple grid layout. As usual, you can find the complete source code of the example in the code examples:

```
<div class="container">
  <div class="row">
  <div class="col-md-8">
    <div class="chart" data-url="…" …>
    </div>
  </div>
  <div class="col-md-4">
    <h2>My Dashboard</h2>
    <p>This is a simple dashboard</p>
  </div>
</div>
<div class="row">
  <div class="col-md-4">
    <div class="chart" data-url="…" …>
    </div>
  </div>
  <div class="col-md-4">
    <div class="chart" data-url="…" …>
    </div>
  </div>
  <div class="col-md-4">
    <div class="chart" data-url="…" …>
    </div>
  </div>
</div>
<div class="row">
  <div class="col-md-6">
    <div class="chart" data-url="…" …>
    </div>
  </div>
  <div class="col-md-6">
    <div class="chart" data-url="…" …>
    </div>
  </div>
</div>
</div>
```

We observe that by making use of the parent containers width, we can simply add the charts as the `div` elements in the columns of the grid. This is the preferred integration where two components play together nicely but are not depended on each other.

In the following figure, we can see a screenshot from the simple dashboard that we just built. We observe that the visualizations already fit nicely into our grid layout, which makes it easy to compose them together:

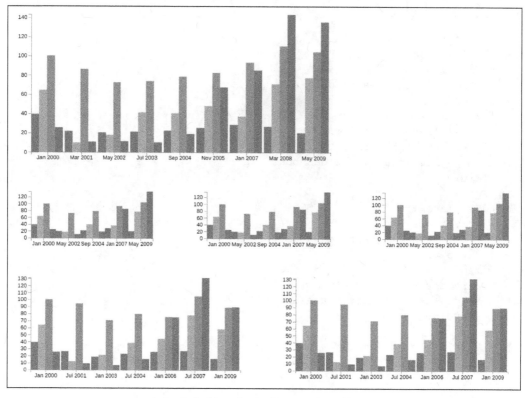

A simple dashboard using Bootstrap's grid layout

Summary

In this chapter, you learned the essentials about absolute and relative units to define lengths in a browser. We remember that the rem unit plays an important role because it allows a layout to adapt when a user increases the font size of the website.

Then, you learned about how to use relative units, viewports, and resize events to adapt the chart size and the data resolution according to the current container size.

In the preceding section, you learned about using Bootstrap Media Queries in CSS, LESS, und JavaScript. Finally, we also saw how to integrate charts with Bootstrap's grid system.

In the next chapter, we will continue with implementing responsive charts and take a closer look at creating responsive interactions for all the types of devices and screen resolutions.

5
Building Responsive Interactions

In the previous chapter, you learned how to make a chart responsive; this means to *look* good on all kind of devices. In this chapter, we will look at responsive interactions; this means to *feel* good on all kind of devices. In this chapter you will learn the following:

- Discovering the D3 event system
- Using native events and the D3 event system
- Understanding responsive interactions
- Implementing interaction targets
- Computing the nearest element of the dataset
- Learning about touch events
- Reviewing mouse events
- Implementing a simple zooming behavior
- Applying complex axis zoom

First, we will look at events in JavaScript and understand how event listeners are used to separate and integrate different components. We will also see the internal D3 event system and learn how to use it. Event systems help to make code cleaner and the execution path easier to follow.

Then, we will look at responsive events and interactions. We will see four different ways to handle interactions on different devices. The most important rule is that we don't use very small interaction targets on small screens.

Then, we will take an overview of native mouse and touch events and their execution order; this will help you to avoid common pitfalls when designing responsive interactions and fully understand when you need to stop events from propagating the default actions.

In the last section of this chapter, we will look at common interaction techniques, such as zooming and panning. We will compare a simple upscaling zoom with a more complex x and y axis zoom in order to understand the difference between the two.

Using an event system

In many of our daily systems and programming languages, the interaction of different instances is handled by events and event listeners (these are also called event handlers or callbacks). Usually, one part of an application or system triggers a certain event and another part of the application or systems — that listens for this event — executes the event listener for the specified event.

Let's think about a simple example in JavaScript. We want to call a resize function whenever a resize event of the browser occurs. Therefore, we have to create an event listener that waits (listens) for the resize event of the browser window and executes the resize() event listener whenever the event occurs. This function is as follows:

```
window.addEventListener('resize', function(event){
  resize();
});
```

This looks quite simple, and it is very easy to understand. The only thing we have to know is which events exist on which elements (in which browsers). You have already learned in a previous chapter that, besides the window element, no other DOM element triggers the resize even. This means that usually, the list of events that can be triggered on elements is standardized and well defined.

Custom events in D3.js

Event systems help to integrate separated components using standardized events. This becomes very handy when it comes to visualizations. You will often find loads of reusable components and parts in a visualization that should be tightly integrated but reusable at the same time.

Think about an axis for example. You will need two of them in a simple 2D chart; however, you will need three of them in a 3D or 2D chart with two y axis. When a user zooms into your chart, the scale of the axis changes in order to display a finer domain of the dataset. At the same time, the displayed data points are also updated. When using events, we can simply listen in all the components for a zoom event and update them accordingly. And the best part is that it doesn't matter if you have two, three, or no axis in your chart; it will still work properly. This means that an arbitrary number of elements (no element or many elements) can automatically listen for events and update when a certain event occurs, and the element that triggered the event doesn't have to know about them. An event system helps you to build clean, modular, and decoupled components that are not directly dependent on each other. This is why I highly recommend you to use one and maybe even D3's event system.

Having this in mind, I encourage you to use an event system and custom events in your visualization in order to standardize the interactions throughout the visualization to keep all the functionality decoupled but integrated. Creating custom events is very easy with D3 because it provides all the necessary functionality.

Let's look at a simple example; here, we want to propagate the `dataClick` event when a user clicks on a bar in the bar chart. First, we need to create a so-called `dispatcher` that knows all the events for a certain component. In our case, we will use one single dispatcher for the whole chart:

```
// Create dispatcher
var dispatch = d3.dispatch("dataClick");
```

A dispatcher is the piece of code that can trigger events. In the preceding code, we initialize a dispatcher that can trigger the `dataClick` event. Besides triggering events, the dispatcher is also used by other components to listen for events.

Next, we create an event listener that is executed whenever the event occurs. This code will usually be placed in a reusable component that we want to separate from the chart (axis, grid, legend, minimap, and more):

```
// Register an event listener
dispatch.on("dataClick", function(args){
  console.log("Data clicked", args);
});
```

In the preceding code, we see that we only need to access the dispatch object to register an event listener. It's very common that the method to listen for an event is called on and has the signature called `.on(eventName, eventHandler)`. We listen for the `dataClick` event and register an event handler (also called callback or event listener) that logs the argument to the console. Note that we always need to make sure that the component provides a way for other components to register event handlers and hence to to access the dispatch object.

Finally, we can trigger the event by simply calling the event as a function on the dispatcher object:

```
// Dispatch event
dispatch.dataClick({foo: 'bar'});
```

We see in the preceding code that we can also send some data together with the event. After triggering the event, all event listeners of this event will be executed with the event data as argument.

Again, D3's event system is perfect to create an event-based architecture for your visualization, and I really encourage you to do so. This makes it much easier to trace function calls through the application, create reusable, and decoupled components, and standardize the communication between the different components.

 You can find more information about the D3 event system on the Github page of the project at `https://github.com/mbostock/d3/wiki/Internals#events`.

Responsive events

Making your visualization appealing on mobile devices does not only mean to make them look good but also to make them feel good or to make them work at all. And an interactive visualization only feels good when you can actually do all the interactions not just with a mouse but also with your fingertip. You learned in the previous chapter that displaying too much data on a low-resolution device is bad because one cannot really differentiate the data points anymore, which leads to poor performance and usability. Another good reason to reduce the resolution of the data for mobile devices is that it automatically makes the interaction areas on the data points bigger.

Interaction areas

While we can draw with pixel precision using a mouse pointer or a digital pencil, we need between 7 mm to 9.5mm targets to successfully interact with them using our fingertips. This area is much bigger than most buttons, data points, and elements on a desktop-optimized application; therefore, interaction with these applications is, most of the time, unsatisfying. We have to keep in mind that if we want a user to interact with the data points in the visualizations, then the interaction area of a data point in the visualization needs to be big enough. In general, there are three methods to achieve this:

- Creating bigger targets—therefore, bigger data points
- Creating big invisible interaction targets at the top of data points
- Always interacting with the closest data point from the finger's position

It's a good rule of thumb to make data points big enough so that you can interact with them using your fingertips; however, in many cases, it is just not possible to scale them up to a radius of 9.5 mm.

The first point is somewhat obvious; we increase the size of all elements in the visualization. While this might result in bigger interaction targets, it might also lead to ugly magnification problems, overlapping data samples, and so on. However, when there is enough space in the visualization, it is a good enough solution.

To minimize magnification errors and overlaps in the visualization, we simply use overlying invisible interaction targets. While this solves the problem of ugly overlapping artifacts, it doesn't solve the problem of overlapping interaction targets. When two targets overlap, a touch event will always be received by the element that has been created the latest, and there is no easy way to change this behavior.

There is no right way to solve the issue of big interaction areas; I, personally, prefer the third point: interacting with the closest data point from the finger's position. Whenever the user touches the visualization, we look up the closest data point to the finger position. We can even combine this technique with the second point of invisible interaction areas around the data. We can estimate if the distance between the finger and the data point center is smaller than 9.5 mm (or some other threshold). This method prevents overlapping artifacts for the data points as well as for the interaction areas; this is a good trade-off but slightly more complicated and computationally expensive.

Creating interaction targets

Let's take a look at these methods and implement them!

The quickest solution is to create interaction targets that are much bigger than the original data points, overlaid on the original element, and transparent. This method doesn't require a lot of changes because you can use standard `click` event handlers on elements, see the elements in the Developer Tools (as before), and inspect the interaction targets by making them visible.

To implement this, you simply need to create circles with a size of 9.5 mm and `opacity` 0. Here, you attach click listeners. You can find an example in the code that is provided with this book. The screenshots of the examples are identical with the ones provided in the following section.

However, in some situations, especially when you deal with many data points, you don't want to spoil your container with interaction elements. Therefore, we want to look at different and more flexible solutions.

Computing the nearest data point

To successfully apply the nearest-point technique, we have to compute the nearest data point from the touch position. Let's think about the steps we will have to apply to obtain the nearest element from a `click` event listener on the `svg` element:

```
$svg.on('click', function(){
  // Get the relative position
  var pos = d3.mouse(this);
  // Computation goes here
});
```

As we can see in the preceding code, we obtain the position of the finger or mouse relative to the `svg` element using the `d3.mouse` function with the `this` argument (which is referencing the current `svg` element). This computes and returns the relative position of the finger or mouse to the reference element. We use the `d3.mouse` function rather than the `d3.touch` or `d3.touches` function to indicate that we are only interested in a single click position (with the finger) rather than a touch gesture of multiple fingers.

 You can find more information about d3.event, d3.mouse, and d3.touches on the Github page of the project at https://github.com/mbostock/d3/wiki/ Selections#d3_mouse.

Next, we need to transform the coordinates of the click position (a value from the pixel range) into the domain of the dataset; this is usually done using the inverse scale operator in D3:

```
var xValue = xScale.invert(pos[0]);
```

In the preceding code, we reused the xScale object that we created in *Chapter 2, Creating a Bar Chart Using D3.js and SVG* in order to map the pixel value to a value in the domain of the x values of the dataset. Now, we need to find the index on which the value of the click position intersects the array of x values in the data set. We can obtain it by iterating the array from the beginning (left) or from the end (right) and comparing the value to the array values. We can also use d3.bisector to create a bisect function that does exactly this:

```
// Create a left bisector
var bisect = d3.bisector(xKey).left;

// Get the index where the intersection occurs
var index = bisect(data, xValue);
```

In the preceding function, we reused the xKey function and data object from *Chapter 2, Creating a Bar Chart Using D3.js and SVG*

> You can find more information about bisectors on the Github page of the project at https://github.com/mbostock/d3/wiki/Arrays#d3_bisector.

Finally, we just have to check whether the index exists (because of the default scale setting for non-clamping scales) and compare whether the current or previous value is closer to the click position:

```
if (index == 0 || index > data.length) {
  return;
}
var d0 = data[index - 1];
var d1 = data[index];
// get the nearest value
var d = xValue - xKey(d0) > xKey(d1) - xValue ? d1 : d0;
```

Finally, d contains the closest entry of the dataset to our click position. In the final step, we check if the data point is closer than a certain threshold:

```
function distance(x0, x1, y0, y1, r){
  r = r || 0;
  return Math.sqrt(Math.pow(x0+r-x1, 2) + Math.pow(y0+r-y1, 2));
```

```
}

var yValue = yScale.invert(pos[1]);
var k = distance(xKey(d), xValue, yKey(d), yValue);
// if k less than 9.5mm
if (k < 9.6/2.54*9.5) {
  // Mark data point as active
}
```

In the preceding code, we defined a distance function that returns the Euclidean distance in 2D, and we applied it to the click position and the center point of the nearest data point; we compared if the distance is less than 9.5 mm (*96/2.54 = 1 cm, 9.6/2.54 = 1 mm*).

In the preceding example, we saw that this gives accurate results according to our definition. However, keep in mind that there is a computation (array iteration/ search) going on while the user clicks on a data point; depending on the amount of data and the size of the dataset, this can lead to a laggy user experience. In this case, we have to use plain simply `click` event listeners on the data points directly.

Let's look at a simple scatter plot with one data series where we can see the preceding code in action. In the following figure, we see such a plot:

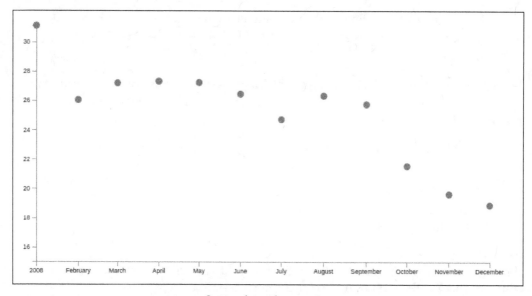

Scatter plot with one series

You can find this example in the code samples bundled with the book. If you now click on the chart next to a data point, the point will automatically get selected. We can see the selected element in the following figure; whenever we click closer than 9.5 mm away from a point, the closest point on the x axis will get selected:

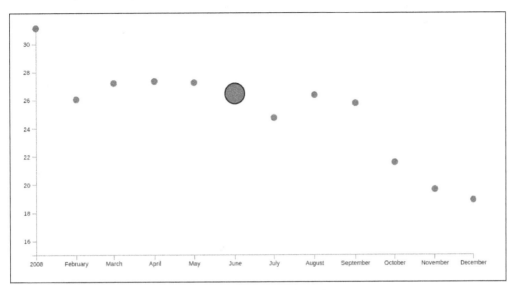

The scatter plot with highlighted element

The following figure highlights interaction areas:

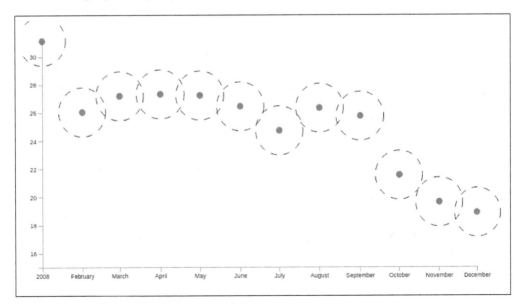

The scatter plot with highlighted interaction areas

The previous solution works great and is commonly used to select the nearest element; however, it has one big caveat. It computes the closest distance only on the x axis, which means that it can't distinguish elements that are closer on the y axis. The biggest problem is dealing with multiple series or more data points with the same x value, such as in the following figure:

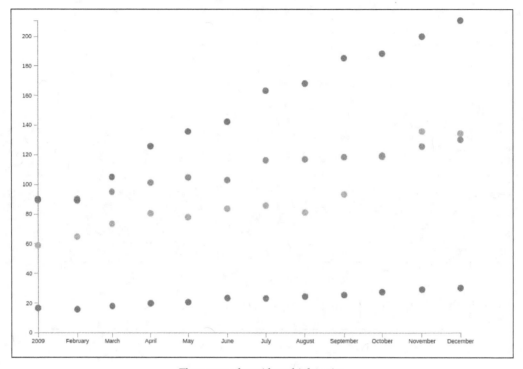

The scatter plot with multiple series

We can solve this using a very naive solution by computing the distance of each data point to the click position in the pixel range and selecting the smallest of those. Let's implement this and create the click event listener on the svg element:

```
$svg.on('click', function(){
  // Get the relative position
  var pos = d3.mouse(this);

  // Computation goes here
});
```

Now, we can transform the data array to an array of distances relative to the click position; we use the distance function from the previous example:

```
var distances = flatData.map(function(d){
  var x = xScale(xKey(d));
```

```
    var y = yScale(yKey(d));
    return distance(x, pos[0], y, pos[1]);
});
```

Now we can selected the minimum distance and the matching element from the dataset.

```
var k = d3.min(distances);

var index = distances.indexOf(k);
var d = data[index];

// if k less than 9.5mm
if (k <= 9.6/2.54*9.5) {
  // Mark data point as active
}
```

If we look at the result, we can see that this solution perfectly handles all the nearest elements through all the series. In the following figure, we see how the nearest element gets selected properly; I encourage you to also try out the sample in the code:

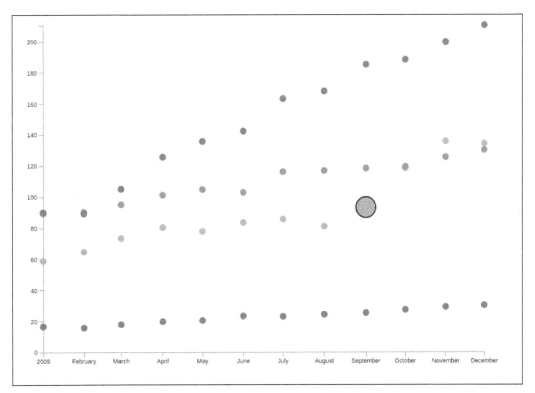

The scatter plot with highlighted element

Let's again display the interaction areas of 9.5 mm; we can see the result in the following figure:

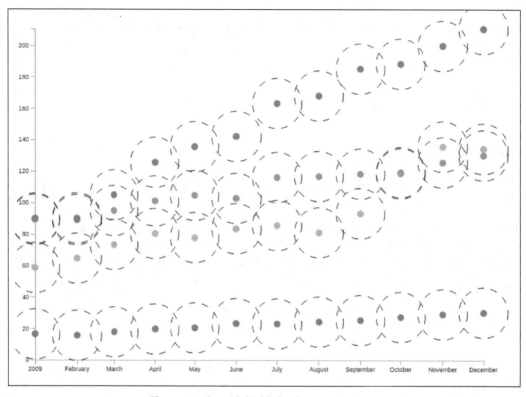

The scatter plot with highlighted interaction areas

While this solution works great with all kinds of data, scales, and axis, because the distance is measured in a pixel range, we need to be aware of calculating the distance of each data point to the click position. Depending on the number of data points, this can lead to performance issues when dealing with big datasets. As always, a mixture of both examples would be a good solution here.

In a performance-compatibility balanced solution, we draw a rectangle around the click position and use bisectors to return all elements of this rectangle. Then, we use the distance function on all elements in this rectangle to obtain the closest one. Using this box method, we only have to compute a fraction of the distances rather than the distance to every point in every dataset. Slicing the dataset with the bisectors is also much faster than computing all distances.

Touch events

Let's take a look at the native event APIs in JavaScript. Here is a list of the most common touch events in their correct execution order:

- `touchstart`: The fingertip touches the screen
- `touchmove`: The fingertip moves on the screen
- `touchend`: The fingertip stops touching the screen
- `touchcancel`: The touch event is canceled

By simply looking at this list, we probably don't understand why our visualization still works perfectly fine for touch input, although we never defined a single `touchstart` event in the code. If we look into the code of the book, we mostly see the `click` events, but how do they get triggered by a touch?

What we don't see in the list is a behavior called emulation handling, which is done automatically by the browser. The browser simply continues to propagate the touch events as emulated mouse events. This means every touch on the screen results in the full touch execution chain as well as the full mouse execution chain; hence, a touch creates a `click` event.

We will take a close look at this execution chain, default handling, and propagations in the last chapter, where you will learn to deal with cross-browser compatibility issues and optimizing for both touch and mouse. Let's continue with the mouse events.

 More information about touch events can be found on MDN at
`https://developer.mozilla.org/en-US/docs/Web/API/Touch_events`.

Mouse events

Mouse events are a little bit more difficult to handle because we have to know not only the names of the events but also the correct execution order (which looks somehow arbitrary at first). Here is a list of the most common mouse events listed by their execution order when users double-click on an element on the screen:

- `mouseenter`: The mouse cursor is entering the element
- `mouseover`: The mouse cursor is hovering the element
- `mousemove`: The mouse is moved over the element
- `mousedown`: The mouse button is pressed
- `mouseup`: The mouse button is released
- `click`: The element is clicked

- `dblclick`: The element is double-clicked
- `mouseleave`: The mouse cursor is leaving the element

As we see, a simple click with the mouse also triggers the `mouseenter`, `mouseover`, and `mouseleave` events. Whenever you deal with events and execution orders, I encourage you to memorize or come back to this list and check the execution chain. Don't forget that you can always stop the propagation and prevent the default event handling using `event.preventDefault()` and `event.stopPropagation()`.

 More information about mouse events can be found on MDN at `https://developer.mozilla.org/en-US/docs/Web/API/MouseEvent`.

Panning and zooming

Besides clicking onto the data points, bars, and elements in the visualization, a common interaction is zooming and panning. This helps the user to change from smaller view to a more detailed view of the data. Having in mind everything you have learned so far, it would also make sense to increase the data resolution while you zoom. The more the user zooms into the visualization, the higher the data resolution.

Similar to the previous chapter, there are multiple ways to implement them. We will look at the different possibilities and compare them by zooming into the chart in the following picture:

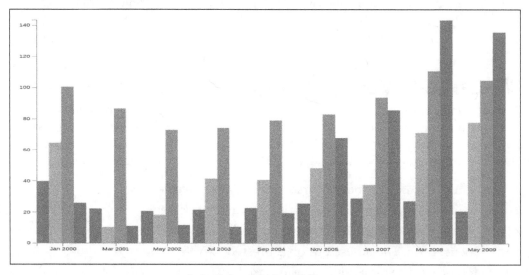

A simple bar chart in a grid layout

A simple zoom

Let's first start with a very simple zoom. In many cases, mostly when we use data representations without axis, we want to provide the user a way to simply enlarge the view of the visualization.

To implement this effect, we can use SVG's native transform functions, such as scale and translate, and apply them to a container element that contains all the zoomable components. We can already see that the zoomable components are not even involved in this technique as long they are placed inside the container. Here lies the great benefit of this method — it is super simple to add to a visualization and very easy to implement.

Let's go through the steps using some more D3 functions. First, we need to make sure all our data is grouped in a visualization container. So, we add a simple container to the chart:

```
var $svg = d3.select(chart).append('svg');
var $vis = $svg.append('g').attr('class', 'vis-container');
var $axesGroup = $vis.append('g').attr('class', 'axis-container');
var $dataGroup = $vis.append('g').attr('class', 'data-container');
```

Next, we initialize a default zoom factor and translation summands. We can use the built-in function called d3.behavior.zoom() to create a zoom generator:

```
var translate = [0,0];
var scale = 1;
var zoom = d3.behavior.zoom()
  .on("zoom", function() {
    translate = d3.event.translate;
    scale = d3.event.scale;
    $vis.attr("transform",
        "translate(" + translate + ")scale(" + scale + ")");
  });
```

In the preceding example, we create a zoom generator function called zoom, which implements a zoom event listener function. When a zoom or pan occurs, we simply scale the visualization container and translate it according to the zooming or panning movement. Finally, we apply the zoom generator to an element:

```
$svg.call(zoom);
```

In our case, we always want the zoom generator on the svg element. That's it, zooming and panning in a couple of lines of code — impressive. And it even handles the pinch-to-zoom action as well as zooming using the mouse wheel and panning (via mouse and fingers).

Let's look at the output of the previous code; the following figure shows the zoomed bar chart using the proposed technique:

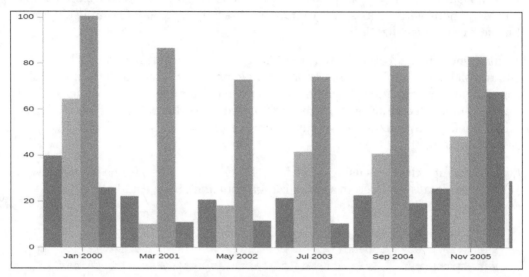

The zoomed bar chart using a simple zoom

We can already see the drawbacks from using this simple function: The zoom is applied on the whole visualization and works similar to the scaling of the graphic. This can be very helpful in a lot of cases, but when we deal with charts it would be more helpful to zoom the data along the axis.

An axis zoom

We can set much more options of the d3.behavior.zoom function and change its behavior by modifying the zoom event listener. We can tell the built-in zooming function that it should use scale objects for zooming and that it should handle all by itself.

In this case, we add xScale and yScale as arguments to the .x() and .y() methods. Therefore, the algorithm overwrites the built-in zoom extend from both the functions every time the draw function is called:

```
var zoom = d3.behavior.zoom()
  .x(xScale)
  .y(yScale)
  .on("zoom", function() {
        // Event listeners goes here
      });
    });
$svg.call(zoom);
```

Finally, add an event handler. In this case, we want to update the axis and the data:

```
$$xAxis.call(xAxis);
$$yAxis.call(yAxis);
nestDataRes.forEach(function(data, i){
  var $$bars = $dataGroup.selectAll('rect.g-' + i)
    .data(data.values, xKey);

  $$bars
    .attr('x', function(d) { return xScale(d.x) + i*barWidth; })
    .attr('y', function(d) { return yScale(d.y); })
    .attr('height', function(d) { return (yScale(0) - yScale(d.y)); })
    .attr('width', barWidth)
    .attr('fill', colors(data.key));
});
```

Let's look at the output of the function in the following figure:

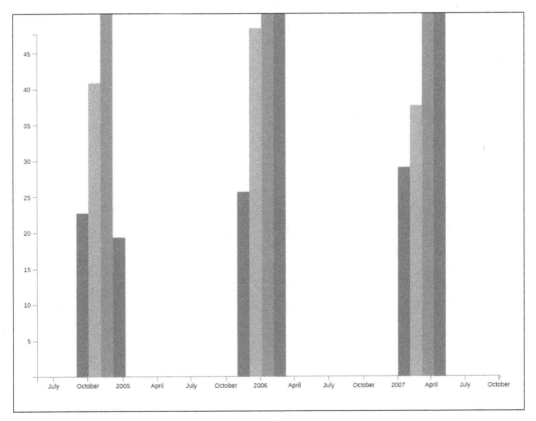

The zoomed bar chart

More information about zoom behavior can be found on the Github page at `https://github.com/mbostock/d3/wiki/Zoom-Behavior`.

Summary

In this chapter, you learned about native events, event listeners, and event systems. We saw that the internal D3 event system is very easy to use, and I strongly recommend you to use it for a visualization tool. It helps to keep your code more organized and follow the execution path through the code.

Then, you learned about interaction targets and how to compute the nearest element using bisectors and using the distances of all the elements relative to the click position.

In the last section, we implemented the common interaction techniques zooming and panning. With D3, these functions are implemented very easily. In the next chapter, you will learn about how to make transitions and animations.

6

Designing Transitions and Animations

In the previous chapters, you learned everything about responsive visualizations and interactions. Now, we want to make them beautiful and bring them to life using transitions and animations. In this chapter, you will cover the following:

- Understanding why we use JavaScript for Web animations
- Implementing a simple animation using D3 timers
- Learning about interpolation function and how they are used in D3
- Learning about easing functions and how they are used
- Understanding the concept of Bézier curves
- Implementing attribute and path transitions
- Understanding the main problems of shape tweens

In the first section, you will learn about different web standards used to animate DOM elements, and you will learn how to compare their advantages and disadvantages for animating visualizations. This will help you understand why we use D3's built-in animations and transitions rather than SMIL or CSS animations.

In the second section, we will cover the main concepts for animations with D3 — timers, interpolations, and easing. We will discover that it is very comfortable to use D3 abstractions to implement custom animations; however, it is too complex for simple transitions.

In the following section, we will see that transitions are actually very easy with D3. We just have to understand what transitions are and how we can construct animations out of transitions.

Finally, you will learn about shape tweens in the last section. It is quite a difficult task, and there is no flexible open source library for shape tweens so far. You will learn about the problems and difficulties in shape tweening and all the necessary information to solve it (and to maybe make an Open Source D3 plugin out of this, just saying).

Is there a web standard for animations?

One of the great things about D3 is that it directly uses underlying standards, such as SVG and CSS, rather than abstracting them with an API. This gives the developer access to all the features that are available within SVG and the web itself. When it comes to animations, one may ask what the web standard for animations is.

In this first section, we will see different ways and technologies that currently exist for animating SVG elements on the web. This will help you to pick the right technology for your application and use case.

Animate SVG using SMIL

Synchronized Multimedia Integration Language(SMIL) is a specification for interactive multimedia content on the web. SMIL animation is a specification for animating DOM elements with an XML syntax that is directly embedded in the DOM tree. Thanks to this, it suits perfectly well to animate SVG visualizations.

SMIL animations for SVG can be constructed using the following elements:

- `<animate>`: This animates a single attribute/property over time
- `<set>`: This sets an attribute/property for a specified duration and is useful for setting non-numeric attribute values in animations
- `<animateMotion>`: This animates an element along a motion path
- `<animateColor>`: This animates a color over time
- `<animateTransform>`: This animate the `tranform` attribute of SVG elements

To animate SVG elements, we simply have to put the SMIL Animation tags inside the element that we want to animate (or use an `xlink:href` attribute to specify the target). Let's look at a simple example. If we want to animate a rectangle along the x coordinate, we can use this:

```
<svg width="800" height="400">
<rect x="50" y="50" width="100" height="100">
<animate attributeName="x" from="50" to="650" dur="1s" />
</rect>
</svg>
```

In the preceding code, we animate the x attribute of the rectangle by placing an `animate` tag inside the `rect` element and defining the attribute that should be animated via the `attributeName` attribute. You can find an animate demo of this example in the code folder.

By defining a `values` attribute instead of the `from` and `to` attributes, SMIL can also interpolate strings properly. This is very useful for animating the path element of SVG paths where the control points are encoded as strings. Using this technique, we can also do shape animations, as shown in the following figure:

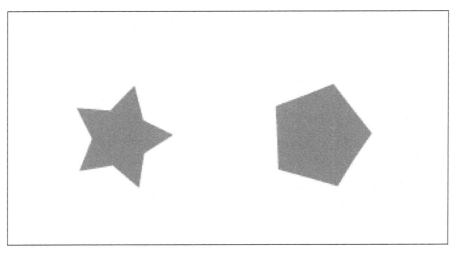

A shape animation

Here is a simple example where we animate the shape of a path:

```
<svg width="800" height="600">
<path>
<animate
      attributeName="d"
      dur="3000ms"
      repeatCount="indefinite"
      values="m 7.3867404,14.177924 -0.7836793,-0.735313
-1.050013,0.228716 0.457154,-0.972548 -0.5419939,-0.927944
1.066216,0.134245 0.7150424,-0.802217 0.2018038,1.055516
0.9839143,0.432147 -0.9414944,0.518099 z;
      M 7.3867404,14.177924 6.476792,13.939795 5.5530481,13.671327
5.497234,12.698779 l -0.029026,-0.927944 0.8847042,-0.331372
0.8965542,-0.3366 0.7068801,0.866112 0.478838,0.621551
-0.5390117,0.802204 z;" />
</path>
</svg>
```

In the preceding code, we transform a star into a hexagon by simply adding both the element paths to the `values` attribute. Note that, in this simple case, the animation looks good because we use the same number of control points for both the shapes. We will discuss this in more detail in a later section of shape tweens.

> You can find the complete SMIL specification on the W3C website at `http://www.w3.org/TR/REC-smil/` and the section about SMIL Animations at `http://www.w3.org/TR/2001/REC-smil-animation-20010904/`. The specification for SMIL SVG Animations can be found at `http://www.w3.org/TR/SVG/animate.html`.

Although, SMIL animations offer a great interface to describe (also complex) SVG animations, let's not get too excited. The following figure shows that SMIL Animations are not supported in Internet Explorer or Edge:

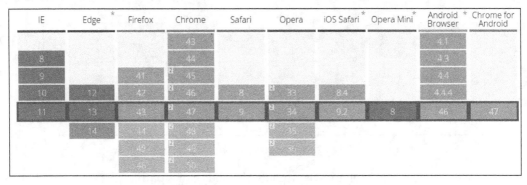

The cross-browser compatibility of SMIL Animations

While the lack of SMIL support in Microsoft products makes it a bad choice for many projects, there is a worst message hidden in the figure. In Chrome, SMIL animations are marked as deprecated since version 45, which means that they can be removed in any of the following versions. The decision of the Chrome team to stop supporting SMIL animations was to establish and strengthen JavaScript and CSS as a web standard for DOM animations. Therefore, developers should also favor web standards, such as CSS and JavaScript, when it comes to animations and transitions.

Animating HTML using CSS

CSS has become the de facto standard for animating DOM elements in recent years. It is mainly used to transform HTML elements over time, but it can also be used to animate the properties of SVG elements.

Animations in CSS are defined via the `@keyframes` keyword. Let's create a similar example as before where we want to move a rectangle from left to right:

```
<style>
  @keyframes move {
    from {x: 50;}
    to {x: 650;}
  }

  rect {
    animation-name: move;
    animation-duration: 1s;
  }

</style>
<svg width="800" height="400">
<rect x="50" y="50" width="100" height="100"></rect>
</svg>
```

The preceding code does the exact same thing as the first example in the previous section. We observe that the animation code in this example has now been separated from the visualization code, which makes the animation code more reusable (just as CSS styles). But it makes it more difficult to write. It is not very intuitive to define key frames and then declare an animation that consists of these key frames.

In the following figure, we see that the support of CSS Animations across all modern browser is pretty decent. However, if we try to animate the path element, similar to the previous example, we soon reach the limits of CSS animations. Interpolations are simply not as good as the ones from SMIL. Moreover, animating the transform attribute in SVG is a nightmare; different transform origins, and the lack of support in Internet Explorer makes them almost unusable:

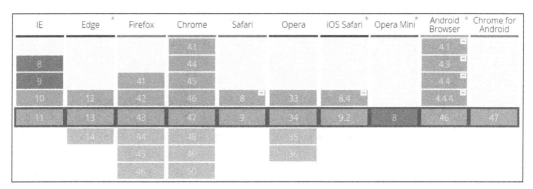

The cross-browser compatibility of CSS Animations

While CSS animations are a good choice for animating and transforming HTML elements, they limit us for creating complex animated visualizations in SVG. When it comes to path interpolations and shape tweens, we better choose an approach in JavaScript.

Animating anything using JavaScript

Are JavaScript Animations the best and most standard way to animate DOM element? Well, not really. They allow all kinds of animations: custom path interpolations, and so on, but they have to explicitly modify the DOM.

Let's try the same example as before where we animate the x position of a rectangle. We therefore, create a little helper function in JavaScript called `animate()`:

```
<svg width="800" height="600">
<rect x="50" y="60" width="100" height="100"></rect>
</svg>
<script>
var rects = document.getElementsByTagName('rect');

animate(rects[0], 'x', 50, 650);

function animate(elem, attributeName, startValue, endValue) {
  var timeStep = 1;
  var valueStep = 5;

  var intervalId = setInterval(function(){
    var value = parseFloat(elem.getAttribute(attributeName));
    elem.setAttribute(attributeName, value + valueStep);

    if (value >= endValue) {
      elem.setAttribute(attributeName, startValue);
      clearInterval(intervalId);
    }
  }, timeStep);
}
</script>
```

In the preceding code, we do the exact same as in the previous example. We animate the x position of the rectangle to move it to the right-hand side. However, as you can see, we have to code everything ourselves, including the handling of the time interval. We can improve the performance of the preceding example using the highest framerate of the browser using the native `window.requestAnimationFrame(callback)` timer. However, whenever we handle timers ourselves, we have to pay extra attention to start, pause and stop them properly.

Hold on, is there something called the Web animations API that would make the preceding code much easier? Yeah, exactly; finally, we understand why SMIL has been deprecated in the Chrome browser. W3C is already working on a specification for a native Web animation API that supports animations natively and provides an easy interface for animations. The specification is still in draft, but it is already a good time to get excited about it, as it will bring a clean interface for animations and a nice performance boost for your JavaScript animations.

Let's see the preceding example with the Web Animation API:

```
<svg width="800" height="600">
<rect x="50" y="60" width="100" height="100"></rect>
</svg>
<script>
var rects = document.getElementsByTagName('rect');

rects[0].animate([
  { x: 50 },
  { x: 650 }
], {
  duration: 1000,
  fill: 'none'
});
</script>
```

In the preceding code, we can see that we get the beautiful declarative way of animations paired with a CSS-like native support directly in JavaScript. This will be the standard way to do animations in the coming years; however, if we look at present (in the following figure), things don't look so good. As I said before, the specification is still in draft, and therefore the browser support is still pretty bad. This means we will have to use the abstraction of JavaScript timers for animation currently, but we should keep this awesome API in our heads:

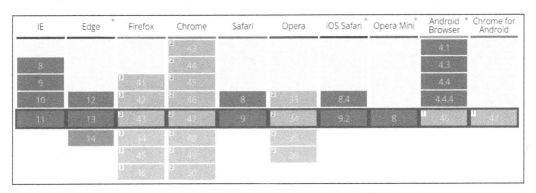

The cross-browser compatibility of the Web Animation API

The full specification and its current status can be found on Github at `https://w3c.github.io/web-animations/`. A nice tutorial about Web Animations can be found on Daniel Wilson's Blog at `http://danielcwilson.com/tags/web-animations-api/`.

Without Web Animations API, we have to implement the timing control ourselves (not a good idea) or rely on animation abstractions from different libraries. jQuery, AngularJS, GreenSock, and so on—they all provide an abstraction for animating DOM elements in JavaScript, but we will use D3 for this purpose. It also provides a powerful abstraction for timers, animations, and transitions that integrates smoothly with the rest of the library. In the following sections, we will see these things in action.

Creating animations with JavaScript

Before discussing animations in JavaScript or D3, we need to make sure what defines an animation. An animation is a timed sequence of transformations on one or multiple elements to create an effect of motion.

Timers and intervals in D3

Animation are timed transitions; therefore, we need to keep track of the time in an animation. If we are dealing with a huge number of elements, we have to manually keep a track of a huge number of timers. Luckily, D3 provides an abstraction for timers and interval function with the `d3.timer(tickFn[, delay[, time]])` method. This timer function calls `tickFn` repeatedly after the relative `delay` or at an absolute date `time` until it returns `true`.

Let's write the previous JavaScript animation example with D3 timers:

```
<svg width="800" height="600">
<rect x="50" y="60" width="100" height="100"></rect>
</svg>
<script>
var rect = d3.select('rect:nth-of-type(1)');

animate(rect, 'x', 50, 650);

function animate(elem, attributeName, startValue, endValue) {
  var valueStep = 5;

    d3.timer(function(time){
```

```
        var value = parseFloat(elem.attr(attributeName));
        elem.attr(attributeName, value + valueStep);

        if (value >= endValue) {
          elem.attr(attributeName, startValue);
          return true;
        }
      });
    }
  </script>
```

In the preceding code, we see only very little changes to the previous example. The most obvious one is that we are now dealing with D3 selections instead of the native HTMLNode objects; this means we can use the .attr() setter and getter methods. However, observe that we replaced the setInterval function with the d3.timer method, which not only removes the need for the intervalId variable to keep track of the timer but also runs automatically at the fastest framerate possible (using requestAnimationFrame() under the hood). We also obtain access to the time variable inside the callback function, which stores the elapsed time in milliseconds since the animation started. Take a look at the code that goes along with the book to find executable examples of these animations.

In the preceding code, we incrementally add the valueStep value to the current x attribute of the rect element. This means we are doing some kind of manual (linear) interpolation of this value. Using D3's timers, we can now easily extend the preceding example to also use D3's interpolations instead of the manual one.

 You can find information about D3 timers on the Github page of the project https://github.com/mbostock/d3/wiki/Transitions#timers.

Interpolating attributes using D3

As we saw in the preceding example, writing the linear interpolations of numeric values is not really difficult even if we want the duration of this interpolation to last for a specific amount of time. It can get tricky if we want to interpolate non-numeric values, such as color values, the coordinates in the d attribute of a path element, or if we want to implement non-linear interpolations (we will see this in the following section about easing).

Let's do a simple example and replace the manual interpolation with a D3 interpolator; we can use the internal function called d3.interpolateNumber(a, b) to create a numeric interpolator between the both numbers called a and b:

```
<svg width="800" height="600">
<rect x="50" y="60" width="100" height="100"></rect>
</svg>
<script>
var rect = d3.select('rect:nth-of-type(1)');

animate(rect, 'x', 50, 650);

function animate(elem, attributeName, startValue, endValue) {
  var duration = 1000;
  var interpolate = d3.interpolateNumber(startValue, endValue);

  d3.timer(function(time){

    elem.attr(attributeName, interpolate(time/duration));

    if (time >= duration) {
      elem.attr(attributeName, startValue);
      return true;
    }
  });
}
</script>
```

In the preceding code, we observe that the valueStep variable is now gone; instead, we use the interpolator function called interpolate(t) generated by the d3.interpolateNumber function. It is a parametric functions that takes the argument called t in the range of [0, 1] to describe the state of the interpolation. Here, 0 corresponds to the initial position and 1 to the final position.

D3 provides the following interpolation generators:

- d3.interpolateNumber: This create an interpolation function for 2 numeric values

- d3.interpolateRound: This creates an interpolation function for 2 numeric values that rounds the result to the nearest integer

- d3.interpolateString: This creates an interpolation function for numbers embedded in a string

- `d3.interpolateRgb`, `d3.interpolateHsl`, `d3.interpolateLab`, `d3.interpolateHcl`: This creates an interpolation function for the specific color space

- `d3.interpolateArray`: This creates an interpolation function for the values in the two arrays that have the same index in both the arrays

- `d3.interpolateObject`: This creates an interpolation function for the properties in the two objects that have the same key in both the objects

- `d3.interpolateTransform`: This creates an interpolation function for two affine transformations, such as translate, rotate, and scale

- `d3.interpolateZoom`: This creates a smooth interpolation function for interpolating two views optimized for smooth zooming and panning

Depending on the attribute values, D3 will select a proper interpolation function if you use D3 transitions—if it corresponds to one of the types in the preceding list. You can even add custom interpolation function by adding the interpolator to the array `d3.interpolators`.

You can find further information about D3 interpolations on the Github page of the project `https://github.com/mbostock/d3/wiki/Transitions#interpolation`.

Easing – Animation progress over time

Until now, we always assumed that we are doing linear interpolations, which means the animation proceeds linear with time. Let's look at the following figure where we animate the position of a circle from the start value of `0.0` to the end value of `1.0`. If the animation has a duration of a second and we take a snapshot every 0.2 seconds, we see the following transition:

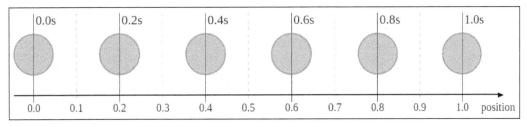

A simple animation with linear easing

We use the term *ease* to describe the relation between the animation process and the animation time; in the preceding figure, we spoke of *linear easing*.

If we look at motions in the real world, we rarely see linear easing; the reason for this is that motion and forces are always damped or accelerated (by gravity). If we want to create physically realistic animations, we have to also add damping or acceleration to our animations. We do so by modifying the easing function of an animation.

The following figure shows a linear easing function; thus, it represents a linear animation's progress over time.

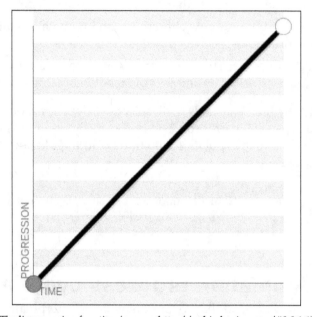

The linear easing function (source: http://cubic-bezier.com/#0,0,1,1)

By modifying the easing function, we can modify the animation progress to create more physically plausible animations. We can make the animation progress faster at the end to simulate acceleration or slow it down to simulate damping.

 Useful information about CSS and JavaScript easing functions can be found at http://easings.net/.

Here comes the part where it may get a little tricky for you. To modify the easing function, we normally use Bézier curves. Well, we could also use some quadratic equations or parabolas and the output would be exactly the same. However, Bézier curves are smooth curves that can be constructed from control points. If you don't care about this, you can safely skip the next section and continue with the other easing functions; however, the concept of Bézier curves will appear more often than you would have expected, so it cannot hurt you to go through the section.

Bézier curves

The goal is to create and handle polynomial functions with ease that correspond to a certain progress over time. Creating linear functions such as the linear easing function that we used in the preceding example is straightforward; you learned this in high school mathematics. However, when we think about quadratic or cubic functions (degree 2 or 3), this gets much more complicated. It's not straightforward anymore to create a function to describe a desired shape.

Let's look at the equation of a cubic polynomial function:

$$f(x) = a \cdot x^3 + b \cdot x^2 + c \cdot x + d$$

Now, I would ask you to find the a, b, c, and d parameters such that the polynomial function goes through the 0,0 point and accelerates towards the 1,1 point. This is similar as the progress of the function in the following figure:

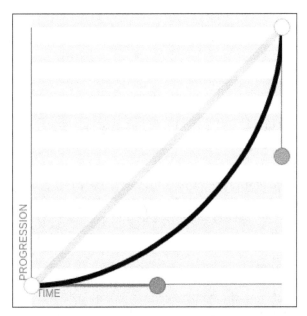

The cubic easing function (source: http://cubic-bezier.com/#.5,0,1,.5)

You will soon find out that, although it is not impossible to create a function for the preceding figure, it is very nasty and not intuitive using a simple polynomial function. The reason for this is that changes of the coefficients a, b, c, or d lead to unpredictable changes of the described function.

Luckily, the clever guys called De-Casteljau and Bézier developed the concept of Bézier curves — a mathematical model for describing polynomial functions by the so-called control points. Bézier curves are parametric polynomial functions that are described by a parameter t in the range of [0, 1] and a certain number of control points (four control points for a polynomial of degree 3). The resulting function is the interpolation between the control points at a position where, at t=0, the function matches the first control point and, at t=1, the function matches the last control point.

The general equation of a Bézier curve is denoted as follows:

$$f(t) = \sum_{i=0}^{n} B_{i,n}(t) \cdot P_i$$

Here, B is the Bernstein polynomial:

$$B_{i,n}(t) = \binom{n}{i} t^i (1-t)^{n-i}$$

The cubic polynomial function from the preceding can now be written as a parametric Bézier curve:

$$f(t) = (1-t)^3 \cdot P_0 + 3t(1-t)^2 \cdot P_1 + 3t^2(1-t) \cdot P_2 + t^3 \cdot P_3$$

Here, P0, P1, P2, and P3 are the control points of the curve. Now, we can create the easing function that we want by simply moving the control points at the desired position and defining the curvature of the polynomial. In the preceding figure of the cubic polynomial, we can see the starting and end points fixed to (0,0) and (1,1) and the 2 remaining control points in turquoise and magenta that define the progress of the easing function.

In the following figure, we can see how a cubic polynomial function can easily be adjusted by simply defining the control points. We also observe that the curve goes through the start and ending points and is smoothly interpolated between the control points. We can also see that the resulting function (in blue) is simply an interpolation between the control points:

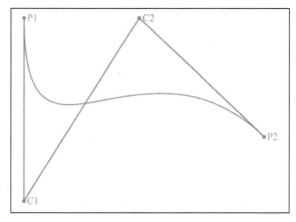

Bézier curve interpolated between the control points

Now, we have the knowledge and tools to write all the possible easing functions that we can think of by simply defining control points and using Bézier curves. The interactive tool from `http://cubic-bezier.com/` allows you to easily create custom Bézier curves and easing effects.

> If you look for the implementations of easing functions rather than Bézier curves, take a look at the jQuery easing plugin by Dan Rogers on Github at `https://github.com/danro/jquery-easing/blob/master/jquery.easing.js`.

Easing functions in D3

D3 supports multiple out-of-the box easing functions that help to make your animations and transitions more plausible. We can create an easing function using the `d3.ease(type)` function. Here, `type` is one of the following easing types:

- `linear`: This is the linear easing function
- `quad`: This is the quadratic easing function
- `cubic`: This is the cubic easing function
- `sin`: This is the sine easing function
- `exp`: This is the exponential easing function
- `circle`: This is the quarter circle easing function
- `bounce`: This is the easing function with the bouncing effect

By default, the easing functions use the easing mode called `in`; this means that the easing motion refers to the element sliding `in` to the target. The easing mode can also be modified by simply appending on the following modes the name of the easing function:

- `in`: element sliding into the target
- `out`: element sliding out of the source
- `in-out`: element sliding out of the source and into the target
- `out-in`: inverse easing of `in-out`

The default easing function is `cubic-in-out`, which corresponds to a slow sliding out and sliding in animation. Let's look at a simply example:

```
<svg width="800" height="600">
<rect x="50" y="60" width="100" height="100"></rect>
</svg>
<script>
var rect = d3.select('rect:nth-of-type(1)');

animate(rect, 'x', 50, 650);

function animate(elem, attributeName, startValue, endValue) {
  var duration = 1000;
  var interpolate = d3.interpolateNumber(startValue, endValue);
  var ease = d3.ease('cubic-in-out');

  d3.timer(function(time) {
    var t = ease(time/duration);
    elem.attr(attributeName, interpolate(t));

    if (t >= 1) {
      elem.attr(attributeName, startValue);
      return true;
    }
  });
}
</script>
```

In the preceding code, we create an easing function by calling the `d3.ease('cubic-in-out')` method. Now, we can use the function to create and modify the `t` parameter for the interpolation function according to the easing type.

The following figure shows an overview and comparison of multiple easing types; you can find an animated example in the code that comes with this book:

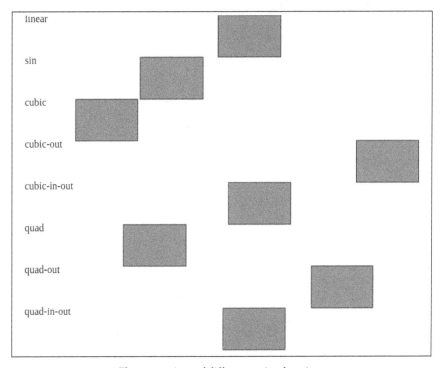

The comparison of different easing functions

>
>
> You can find more information about D3 easing functions on the Github page of the project at https://github.com/ mbostock/d3/wiki/Transitions#d3_ease. A great showcase of D3 easing function can be found on Katsumi Takano's Blocks at http://bl.ocks.org/hunzy/9929724.

Transitions

Until now, you learned a lot about animation, timers, interpolation, and easing, but does it really need all of this to do simple animations in D3. No; luckily, not as long as we use simple transitions. A Transition is an animation from a start state to one end state. The term is often used for animations in general and vice versa, but I want to emphasize that a transition is a simple animation that is defined by two states only; here, the interpolation between these states is automatically created from these states.

D3 has a very powerful support to create transitions. The only thing we have to do is to provide the starting state, call the `.transition()` method on a selection, and finally provide the ending state and D3 will take care of the rest. The `.transition()` method will return an object that is very similar to a selection and has most of its methods. In addition, it provides the `.duration(duration)`, `.delay(delay)`, and `.easing(easingType)` functions to define the duration time, delay time, and the easing type of the transition.

Great, let's see an example where we use transitions instead of custom animations:

```
<svg width="800" height="600">
<rect x="50" y="60" width="100" height="100"></rect>
</svg>
<script>
var rect = d3.select('rect:nth-of-type(1)');

animate(rect, 'x', 50, 650);

function animate(elem, attributeName, startValue, endValue) {
  elem
  .attr(attributeName, startValue)
  .transition()
  .duration(1000)
  .attr(attributeName, endValue);
}
</script>
```

In the preceding code, we can see how easy it is to implement animations as simple transitions in D3. Depending on the `startValue` and `endValue` attributes, D3 tries to figure out which interpolation method it needs to use to create the animation.

Let's look at the code from our bar chart component; here is the snippet to remember the most important part where we update the dimensions of the bars:

```
$$bars
  .attr('x', function(d) { return xScale(d.x) + i*barWidth; })
  .attr('y', function(d) { return yScale(d.y); })
  .attr('height', function(d) { return (yScale(0) - yScale(d.y)); })
  .attr('width', barWidth)
  .attr('fill', colors(data.key));
```

Let's add a little tweak, so the bars automatically update with a nice animation. Using transitions, we only have to define a starting and ending state:

```
$$bars
  .attr('x', function(d) { return xScale(d.x) + i*barWidth; })
  .attr('y', function(d) { return yScale(0); })
```

```
    .attr('height', 0)
    .attr('width', barWidth)
    .attr('fill', colors(data.key));

$$bars
  .transition()
  .attr('y', function(d) { return yScale(d.y); })
  .attr('height', function(d) { return (yScale(0) - yScale(d.y)); });
```

That's it. In the preceding code, we set the default height of the bar to 0 and its y value to 0 in the value range. Then, we simply animate both the values to create a nice animation. In the following figure, we can see how the chart gets updated and the bars seem to grow in a nice animation:

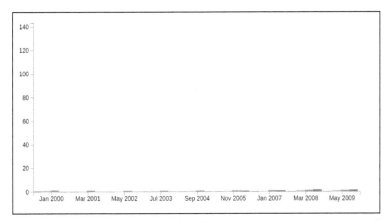

A chart with update transition

After the default transition duration of 250 ms, the chart looks as follows — all the bars have the final height. You can find the animated example in the source code:

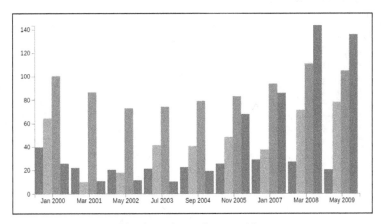

The chart after update transition

Path transitions made easy

If we use D3's path generators, it is also quite simple to animate shapes. We can define the starting state as one generator and the ending state as another generator for the transition, and D3 will do the rest for us. Let's look at an example:

```
<svg width="800" height="600">
<path class="area" />
</svg>

<script>

var $path = d3.select('.area');
var points = [
  [0,0], [100, 10], [200, 250],
  [300, 375], [400, 340], [500, 135],
  [600, 360], [700, 280], [800, 480]
];

var area0 = d3.svg.area()
  .y0(600)
  .y1(600)
  .x(function(d) { return d[0]; })
  .tension(1.0)
  .interpolate('cardinal');

var area1 = d3.svg.area()
  .y0(600)
  .y1(function(d) { return 600 - d[1]; })
  .x(function(d) { return d[0]; })
  .interpolate('cardinal')
  .tension(0.6);

$path.datum(points)
  .attr('d', area0)
  .transition()
  .duration(1000)
  .attr('d', area1);

</script>
```

In the preceding example, we define a path SVG element and an array of coordinates in JavaScript. Then, we create area generators called `area0` and `area1`. We can now animate between both similar shapes using the first area generator called `area0` as the starting state and `area1` as the ending state. The following figure shows a snapshot of the area after first couple of milliseconds:

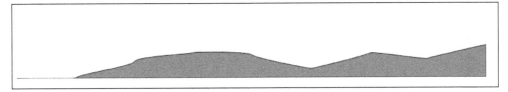

An area with update transition

Finally, the area will smoothly animate to the one shown in the following figure; and all we have to do is to define the starting and ending state:

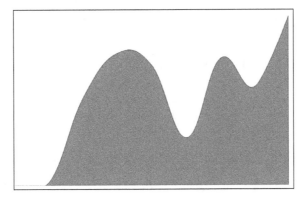

The area after update transition

I want to emphasize that the preceding animation only looks good because both shapes are similar. They have the same number of points. If the number of points was different, the built-in string interpolation would not produce beautiful results but some ugly artifacts, due to the interpolation problem (we will discuss this in the final section of this chapter).

Attribute and style tweens for custom interpolation

Whenever the built-in interpolations don't work for us, we can always use custom interpolation function for the state transitions. These custom interpolation functions are called *tweens*, and they are available via the `.tween()`, `.attrTween()`, and `.styleTween()` methods.

The two latter functions are useful when you want to apply custom interpolation functions for certain attributes or styles, whereas the `.tween()` function lets you create a more general tween factory. A tween is a function that must return an interpolation function in the form `function(t) { ... }`.

Let's look at a simple example where we create a custom tween that creates a matrix-like character animation:

```
<svg width="800" height="600">
<text x="10" y="5x0"></text>
</svg>

<script>
var textTween = function(value){
  var l = value.length;
  var randomString = function(length) {
    if (length === 0) {
      return "";
    }
    // generates a random string
    // @src: http://stackoverflow.com/a/10727155
    return Math.round((Math.pow(36, length + 1) - Math.random() *
Math.pow(36, length))).toString(36).slice(1);
  }
  return function() {
    return function(t) {
      var i = Math.floor(t * l);
      var s = value.substr(0, i) + randomString(l - i);
      this.textContent = s;
    }
  };
}

d3.select('text')
  .transition()
  .duration(2500)
  .ease('linear')
  .tween('text', textTween('Welcome to the matrix...'));
</script>
```

In the preceding code, we set up an SVG `text` element and create a transition with a custom tween function that is returned from the `textTween()` call. As mentioned already, the tween function must return an interpolation function. In our interpolation function, we create an index variable called `i`, which contains the index of the string called `value` at the current parameter called `t` in the range of `[0, 1]`. The index starts at `0` and goes up to the total length of `value`. Then, we fill up the remaining characters with a random string. Finally, we write the result into the `textContent` property of the raw HTML node element, which can be accessed via the `this` keyword. We can also observe that we use the `linear` easing instead of the default `cubic-in` easing to make the animation duration equal for each character. It's nice to see that, when writing tweens, we can use all the transition functions that we saw in the previous section.

 You can find more information about their usage in the D3 documentation on Github at `https://github.com/mbostock/d3/wiki/Transitions#attrTween`.

Chained transitions

If we want to build a series of transitions, we can chain transitions together. With D3, it is much easier to create a custom animation as a series of chained transitions rather than a custom animation using timers and interpolators.

Using the `.transition()` method on a transition object instead of a selection, we create a new chained transition that automatically starts after the previous transition has stopped. To be more precise, it overrides the delay value of the transition to begin after the previous transition stopped.

Let's see a simple example:

```
<svg width="800" height="600">
<rect width="100" height="100" />
</svg>

<script>
d3.select('rect')
  .attr('x', 10)
  .attr('y', 10)
  .attr('fill', 'steelblue')
  .transition()
    .duration(1000)
    .attr('fill', 'red')
    .attr('x', 500)
```

```
      .transition()
        .duration(2500)
        .attr('fill', 'green')
        .attr('y', 500)
      .transition()
        .duration(5000)
        .attr('fill', 'steelblue')
        .attr('x', 10)
        .attr('y', 10);
    </script>
```

The preceding animation works really well where each state is animated after each other. However, we need to be aware that only the internal delay attribute was overwritten for each state, so we cannot really use the .delay() method unless we keep track of the previous transition durations.

D3 triggers the end event whenever a transition is finished; we can use this event to control the animation states. Here is an example using the end event:

```
d3.select('rect')
  .attr('x', 10)
  .attr('y', 10)
  .attr('fill', 'steelblue')
  .transition()
    .duration(1000)
    .attr('fill', 'red')
    .attr('x', 500)
    .each('end', function(){
      d3.select(this)
      .transition()
        .duration(2500)
        .attr('fill', 'green')
        .attr('y', 500)
        .each('end', function(){
          d3.select(this)
          .transition()
            .duration(5000)
            .attr('fill', 'steelblue')
            .attr('x', 10)
            .attr('y', 10);
        });
    });
```

The preceding example works better because a new transition gets started whenever an old one has stopped. However, the nested `callback` tree looks really ugly and bears potential errors for your productive code.

One step towards fully chainable transitions is to add a little extension to D3 that allows Promised-based state transitions. Promises are asynchronous representations for future values and have a very nice property — they can be chained together in a flat structure instead of a nested tree structure.

Here is the helper function for Promised-based transitions, which uses an ES6 Promise polyfill to work in all browsers (you can read more about polyfills and their purpose in the last chapter of this book):

```
function add$transition(selection) {
  selection.$transition = function(animationFn) {
    var getPromiseTransition = function() {
      return new Promise(function(resolve, reject) {
        selection.transition()
          .call(animationFn)
          .each("end", function(){
            resolve(selection);
          });
      });
    }
    if (selection.$progress === undefined) {
      selection.$progress = getPromiseTransition();
    }
    else {
      selection.$progress = selection.$progress
        .then(function(){
          return getPromiseTransition();
        });
    }
    return selection;
  }
}
```

Let's go through the preceding code. First, we add a new `.$transition(animationFn)` method to the D3 selection, which allows us to create Promise-based async transitions. Next, we jump to the line where we check if there already exists a `$progress` property on the selection; this property will always store the most recent Promise. If it doesn't exist, we initialize it with a new transition Promise; otherwise, we return a new transition Promise from the `.then()` method, which gets executed after the Promise is resolved. Then, we override the `$progress` property with the result that will be returned from the `.then()` method, which is the most recent Promise.

The get PromiseTransition() function creates a new transition object on the current selection and resolves when the end event is triggered. All the transitions that are applied in the animationFn are applied to this state. Now, we can write the example from before as follows:

```
var $rect = d3.select('rect');

$rect
  .attr('x', 10)
  .attr('y', 10)
  .attr('fill', 'steelblue')
  .call(add$transition);

$rect
  .$transition(function(s){
    s.duration(1000)
    .attr('fill', 'red')
    .attr('x', 500);
  })
  .$transition(function(s){
    s.duration(2500)
    .attr('fill', 'green')
    .attr('y', 500);
  })
  .$transition(function(s){
    s.duration(5000)
    .attr('fill', 'steelblue')
    .attr('x', 10)
    .attr('y', 10);
  });
```

This is beautiful. We now have a fully functional and encapsulated chainable transitions. However, note that this is only one example of how event-based chaining can be combined with Promises to create a true state-based animation. There may be more elegant ways to do this.

 You can find more information about ES6 Promises on the MDN at https://developer.mozilla.org/ en-US/docs/Web/JavaScript/Reference/Global_ Objects/Promise.

Shape tweens

Shape tweens are the holy grail of transitions. I want you to remember the D3 Show Reel available at `http://bl.ocks.org/mbostock/1256572` in 2011 by Mike Bostock—the author of D3. Here, he shows some awesome shape tween capabilities of D3 by transforming a chart into different representations.

Although a shape tween looks very simple and intuitive, they are almost never easy to create. Why is this so? Because the tools such as SMIL and D3 use simple string interpolation function, which extracts the numeric values of a string and interpolates them to the end state. And as soon the end state string looks different form the starting state—it could have a different amount of points, control points, or path commands—the resulting transition won't look good/smooth. Coming back to the D3 Show Reel, most of the transitions that we see are shape tweens of similar shapes—shapes with the same amount of control points.

This is true in particular for tweening between arbitrary shapes and writing reusable tweening functions. If you consider to only prototype a tween from one specific shape to another one, you can also come up with a quick and dirty solution for your case.

Unfortunately, there isn't any open source shape tween library/d3 plugin that can handle all kinds of shapes. This would be a task that such a plugin would have to master the following:

- Converting all the shape elements such as `rect`, `ellipse`, `polygon`, and more into the path elements; only path elements can be seamlessly interpolated

- Converting all the segments of the shape into cubic Bézier curves; with these curves, we can create arbitrary shapes

- Subdividing segments in the starting/ending path to obtain the same number of control points in both shapes; only the shapes with the same number of points can be interpolated seamlessly

- Align the points of the starting shape to the closest point in the ending shape to make the transition look smoother

- Using any string interpolation method, such as `d3.interpolate`, to interpolate both the strings of the shapes

- Optimizing the function that runs under 16ms to look good at 60FPS

If you are keen to work on a plugin such as this, let me know.

There exists another nice way to solve the problem of shape tweening. Instead of creating an interpolation function that does all the work behind the scenes, Christophe Viau came up with the idea to write a D3 plugin for the so-called Superformula shapes. These are complex shapes that can all be constructed using the Superformula—a more general version of the Superellipse formula—and six parameters. The property of these shapes is that they all are constructed by exactly the same amount of line segments, which makes them perfect for smooth interpolation. In the following figure, we can see some of the shapes that can be constructed by this formula and can be used for smooth tweening:

The shapes constructed by Superformula (source: http://bl.ocks.org/mbostock/1020902)

You can find the D3 Superformula plugin on Github at `https://github.com/d3/d3-plugins/tree/master/superformula` and an example on Mike Bostock's Blocks at `http://bl.ocks.org/mbostock/1020902`.

Summary

In the first section, you learned about web standards for animations that although SMIL is pretty cool and powerful, we should start to use CSS and especially JavaScript animations. SMIL animations are deprecated in Chrome, and the specification for Web Animation (JavaScript) API is in progress.

In the following section, you learned how D3 timers abstract the native `setInterval` function and how we can use and built custom interpolations and easing functions. Finally, we saw how to build beautiful animations in D3 by the use of transitions. Transitions are automatic animations between two predefined states: a starting and an ending state. By chaining transitions together, we can again create animations.

In the last section, you learned about shape tweens and the problems of using it on custom shapes. String interpolation functions are dumb, so they only work for similar shapes (shapes with the same amount of control points). We will need to transform and subdivide shapes in order to do proper shape tweening.

In *Chapter 7, Creating Maps and Cartographic Visualizations Using GeoJSON*, you will learn about cartographic visualization and geographic data, such as GeoJSON. We will also make use of all techniques that we have understood so far.

7
Creating Maps and Cartographic Visualizations Using GeoJSON

In the previous chapter, you learned about transitions and animations; now, think about animating features on geographic visualization because we will take a look at cartographic visualization and GeoJSON. In this chapter, you will learn the following:

- Understanding the different challenges of cartographic visualizations
- Understanding the geometric coordinate system
- Learning about the GeoJSON format
- Understanding the problems of GeoJSON and the advantages of TopoJSON
- Learning about 3D to 2D projections
- Getting familiar with helpful tools for cartographic visualizations
- Creating color scales
- Drawing GeoJSON features
- Loading multiple resources at once
- Drawing geographic grids
- Implementing different types of geographic visualizations

In the first section, we will look into the ecosystem of cartographic visualizations and understand different challenges and problems that occur when dealing with such visualizations. First, we will look at geographic coordinate systems, then we will think about how to project the globe into a 2D plane.

In the next section, we will investigate which kind of data we can plot on maps and how to use this geographic data in the browser. Naturally, we will look into GeoJSON and the representation of geographic features in more detail. Then, we will discuss the problems of GeoJSON and how they can be solved using TopoJSON.

In the following section, you will get familiar with multiple tools and techniques, which are useful for cartographic visualization. We will implement color scales, use the geographic shapes generator to generate a path out of GeoJSON features, and look at the Queue.js module to load multiple resources at once.

Finally, we will create different types of cartographic visualization, such as symbol maps and Choropleth maps. I am sure you will enjoy this section, because you will be able to use all the previously learned techniques to create beautiful visualizations on maps.

Overview of cartographic visualizations

The goal is to display cartographic data on an interactive and responsive visualization using D3.js similar to the following example:

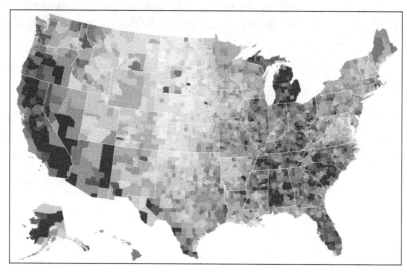

The Choropleth map of USA (source: http://bl.ocks.org/mbostock/4060606)

However, this is not a straightforward task such as drawing a simple bar chart. There are many things that need to be considered when building a cartographic visualization, and this section will introduce you to these different steps and techniques. Let's get started straightaway and look at all the different components from a bar chart and how they can be compared to a cartographic visualization. This will give us enough knowledge on how to tackle the problem.

A geographic coordinate system

When we draw a bar chart, we usually start by drawing a *coordinate system*—a Cartesian coordinate system to be precise—usually represented as axes. This coordinate system defines how we can find the desired coordinates to draw a bar; it shows us the x and y directions on which we can move along. The second important aspect of the axes is that they define the scale of the chart: how close the points from the data set have to be drawn as pixel values in the chart.

When we transform the concept of axes to cartographic visualizations, we need to think about the coordinate system that we use to represent geographic points. The standard way to represent points on a certain location of the world (and hence also in a map) is by latitude, longitude, and elevation. In general, we won't consider the altitude of points on the earth and thus only use the first two for geographic visualizations.

Both latitude and longitude are measured in angles. Latitude is measured in the range of [90°N; 90°S] from the equator (in segments called Parallels), and longitude is measured in the range of [180°W; 180°E] from the prime meridian (in segments called meridians). The following figure compares both measurements and displays circles of equal latitude and longitude. The grid that is formed by equal latitude and longitude is also called graticule:

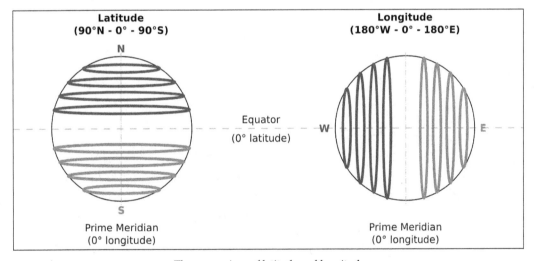

The comparison of latitude and longitude

Projecting a sphere on a flat map

Now, we know how we can precisely identify any point on the surface of the world. But when it comes to visualizing these points in a flat map, there comes another problem. If we want to display a 2D representation of the world (or a sector of it), we have to project the 3D sphere on a 2D plane. The good news is that this can be done; however, the bad news is that this is not possible without distorting the representation.

When I was in primary school, I was always impressed by the huge size of Antarctica in my school atlas, which looked similar to the following figure. However, my imagination of the big continent was rectified a few years later when I first heard about *geographical projections* and how the 3D world can be mapped into a 2D page in a book:

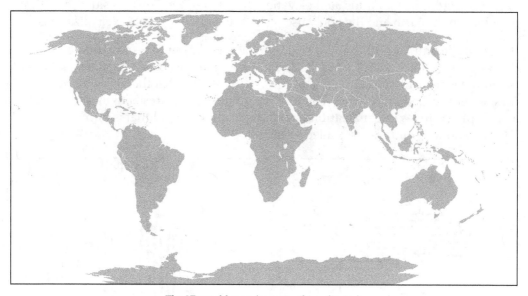

The 2D world map (source wikimedia.org)

The reason for my misconception at the younger age was that I was not aware of the distortion that occurred from projecting the world into a 2D map. In the following figure, we see the real size of Antarctica in comparison with the other continents. As a conclusion, we can say that certain properties, such as the equality of areas, equality of angles, distances, and so on, can get lost when projecting a sphere onto a plane:

The 3D world map (source wikimedia.org)

Which data can be displayed on a map?

With bar charts, line charts, scatter plots, and pie charts, we can display all kinds of 1D, 2D, and 3D data. The dimensions can be encoded as numeric values, time, categorical values, and more and can be represented as dimensions on axis, the size of the data point, and colors. However, when dealing with geographic visualizations, we will mostly deal with 2D data where one dimension represents the location on the map and the remaining dimension represents a value (could be either numerical or ordinal) as a color according to a certain color scale.

There are multiple ways to encode locations:

- ID values can represent continents, countries, states, cities, and so on
- Latitude and longitude coordinates can represent a point on the map
- The coordinates of a polygon can represent an area on the map

To represent a value dimension on this specific location on the map, we most often use a color palette and color the data points according to a predefined color range. However, you should be aware that using color palettes to display numeric values is somehow ambiguous because we perceive color changes differently from size changes. In addition, the designer can control the perception of the user by picking a certain color palette. In the next figure, for example, we see three different visualizations that all display the same data with different color palettes. Whereas, the left and right visualizations look very similar and give the user a similar understanding of the data, the visualization in the middle gives a completely different and contradictory image of the data. This is achieved by simply inverting the color palette from the left visualization. Also, the quantization of the color steps can have a huge impact. In one example, we could generate a very smooth gradient; but with a different quantization, we could create visible borders between the quantizations:

Displaying the same data using different color palettes

It's up to the designer to choose a color palette that goes along with the data that visualizes the aspects one wants the user to see and understand.

Can we start now?

Now, you will have a good overview of which parts and components are needed to draw cartographic visualization. In the following chapters, we will go into details and implement some visualizations using D3.

The only part we have not discussed until now is where we can get the data for geographic visualization and in which format the data is encoded. We will discuss this right ahead in the following section.

Data representation for topology and geographic features

Geographical data is usually stored in databases and programs called **Geographic Information Systems (GIS)**. These are usually tools to design, store, manipulate, analyze, and display the cartographic data. The following figure shows how the different aspects of the world can be abstracted as layers and managed in such a system:

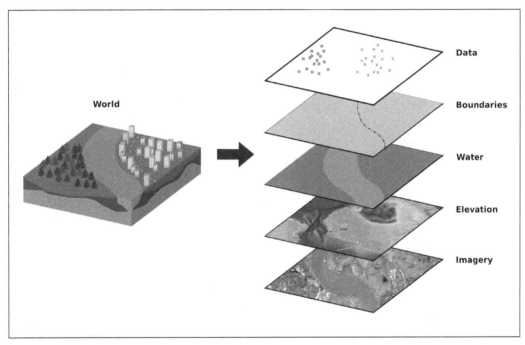

A typical GIS abstraction

Most of these systems provide an interface to access or download these layers separately—that is, cartographic data, statistical data, or other geographic data—in a specified GIS format. There exists a variety of different GIS pixel- and vector-based formats; however, we will look into two JSON-based vector formats: GeoJSON and TopoJSON.

If you are looking for geographic data sets, I recommend you to visit http://www.data.gov/, http://geocommons.com/ as well as the extensive list on Robin Wilson's page at http://freegisdata.rtwilson.com/.

GeoJSON – a format for geographic features

JSON is a great data format for JavaScript, and it works nicely together with D3. So, the only natural choice is to use a JSON format for geographic data, and this is exactly what GeoJSON is.

GeoJSON is a very flexible format that can encode anything from the geometries, features, and collections of features. Let's jump directly into it and take a look at a typical GeoJSON file:

```
{
  "type": "FeatureCollection",
  "features": [
    {
      "type": "Feature",
      "geometry": {
        "type": "Point", "coordinates": [102.0, 0.5]
      },
      "properties": {
        "prop0": "value0",
        "prop1": {"count": 3}
      }
    }, {
      "type": "Feature",
      "geometry": {
        "type": "LineString",
        "coordinates": [
          [102.0, 0.0], [103.0, 1.0], [104.0, 0.0], [105.0, 1.0]
        ]
      },
      "properties": {
        "prop0": "value1",
        "prop1": {"count": 2}
      }
    }, {
      "type": "Feature",
      "geometry": {
        "type": "Polygon",
        "coordinates": [
          [ [100.0, 0.0], [101.0, 0.0], [101.0, 1.0],
            [100.0, 1.0], [100.0, 0.0] ]
        ]
      },
      "properties": {
```

```
        "prop0": "value2",
        "prop1": {"count": 1}
      }
    }
  ]
}
```

In the preceding code, we can see a feature collection where every feature contains a geometry, some properties, and a type. In GeoJSON, a feature collection consists of features with properties and a certain geometry, whereas geometries are constructed out of a few basic elements, such as Points, Lines, and Polygons.

The following are some valid types in GeoJSON:

- Point
- MultiPoint
- LineString
- MultiLineString
- Polygon
- MultiPolygon
- GeometryCollection
- Feature
- FeatureCollection

Whenever we deal with custom data, we will use FeatureCollection as the array of features. However, other types are also possible.

 You can find the complete GeoJSON specification at http://geojson.org/geojson-spec.html.

We can load GeoJSON exactly as we would load a normal JSON file within D3 with the d3.json function. Let's look at an example:

```
d3.json("data/default.json", function(error, data) {
  if (error) throw error;

  console.log(data.features);
});
```

In the preceding code, the data now contains the exact same object that we saw in the preceding example. Now, we only have to extract the relevant information from the data. We obtained the desired properties using a map function:

```
d3.json("data/default.json", function(error, data) {
  if (error) throw error;
  var labels = data.features.map(function(d){
    return d.properties.prop0;
  });
  var values = data.features.map(function(d){
    return d.properties.prop1.count;
  });
});
```

In the preceding code, we use map to transform and extract the relevant properties, such as `values` and `labels`, from the feature collection's `properties` attribute. Note that the shape of the properties object is not standardized and depends on the data structure of your API. In our case, it contains the `prop0` and `prop1` attributes, but it could also contain other attributes. If one of the properties would contain a nested objected, we could also use the `reduce` function to aggregate these values.

It is important to know that we always have to extract the values out of the properties object in order to visualize them.

TopoJSON – GeoJSON for web visualizations

TopoJSON is a format optimized for compressed GeoJSON topology data specified and developed by Mike Bostock, the main author of `D3.js`. It was developed to reduce the size of big GeoJSON files in order to speed up web visualizations.

As we saw in the previous section, the GeoJSON format stores a topology as a list of polygon points; however, any in-land border often belongs to multiple countries or states. Thus, encoding the states' bounding boxes as polygon points leads to (a lot of) redundant information. According to Mike Bostock, a TopoJSON file is 80% smaller than the original GeoJSON file:

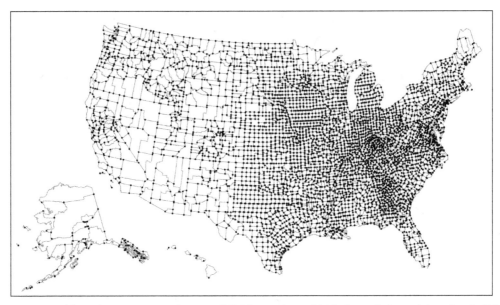

Polygons and boundaries represented as TopoJSON (source https://github.com/mbostock/topojson/wiki)

TopoJSON consists of a server API responsible for converting GeoJSON files into the TopoJSON format, which is available as a command-line tool for node.js and a client API for converting the TopoJSON file back into GeoJSON in the browser.

 You can find more information about TopoJSON on the Github page of the project at https://github.com/mbostock/topojson/wiki/API-Reference.

GeoJSON to TopoJSON via the server API

You can install the TopoJSON server API via the package manager called **npm**; simply run the following from the command line:

```
npm install topojson
```

Finally, when you have the tool installed, you can use it with the following syntax to convert a GeoJSON file called input_geo.json into a TopoJSON file called output_topo.json:

```
topojson -o output_topo.json  input_geo.json
```

 You can find the complete reference for the command-line tool on the Github page of the project at https://github.com/mbostock/topojson/wiki/Command-Line-Reference.

TopoJSON to GeoJSON via the Client API

Once you converted a GeoJSON file into a small TopoJSON file, you also need to convert it back in the browser. Therefore, we have to use the client API, which can be installed either via **bower** (recommended) or **npm** or loaded directly from http://d3js.org/topojson.v1.min.js.

In the browser, we only have to include the script in the header:

```
<script src="bower_components/topojson/topojson.js"></script>
```

Then, we can already use the topojson object.

We can access features and meshes from the original GeoJSON file by calling the following:

- topojson.feature(topology, object)
- topojson.mesh(topology, object, [filter])

Now, we can profit from the huge reduction in the topology file without losing information about the features or meshes. I advise you to always process your input files in such a manner that they stay small and compact in size; TopoJSON is a great way to achieve this.

Maps and projections

As we already saw in the first section of this chapter, there are multiple possible ways of mapping a 3D world into a 2D plane; whereas in all of these methods, some information is lost.

Let's make a little brain experiment. Think about what you would have to do to map the surface of a sphere into the plane. First, you would have to pick a hole somewhere into the surface. Then, you could stretch the surface as long it fits into the plane. However, we introduce a topology violation now at the exact point where we picked the hole. We can easily see that if you move outside of the left side of the map, you should theoretically enter on the right side again; but in our 2D representation, we lost this property, and the two sides are no longer connected. The second problem is that we also introduced a distortion when stretching the surface into the plane. Now, the top and bottom regions in the map seem to be bigger; we could not preserve the equality of the areas. If you look back at the first section at the figure *2D world map*, you can actually see these exact problems.

One could have the great idea of copying the whole 3D sphere into a plane — like in the *3D world map* figure in the first section. However, we only see one side of the sphere here; and hence, we loose all the information about the other side.

This mapping of a sphere to a plane is called projection. D3 offers a variety of built-in projections for all kinds of mappings, available under the d3.geo namespace.

 You can find more information about maps on Mike Bostock's blog at http://bost.ocks.org/mike/map/.

The Equirectangular projections

Remember the brain experiment we just did before? To create such a simple projection in D3, we can use the d3.geo.equirectangular() function that preserves neither distances nor areas. It is the most basic projection because parallels and meridians are simply mapped to parallels and normals in a Euclidean space. We can see the previously discussed distortion effects in the following figure:

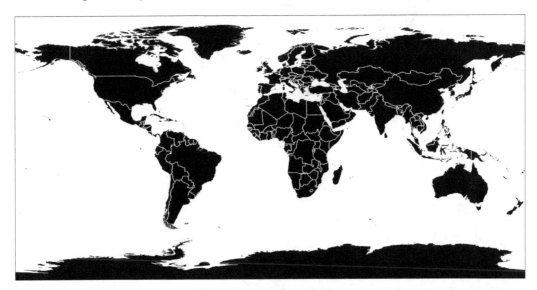

The Equirectangular projection

Due to the fact of not preserving areas, angles, or distances, it is rarely used for visualizing geographic features. However, it is used sometimes for raster reprojection of pixel values to other representations.

Orthographic projection

Now, we continue the brain experiment from before. Let's move to a 3D projection onto a 2D plane, which is called orthographic projection. As we can see in the following figure, when using orthographic projection, we lose the information about one side of the sphere:

The Orthographic projection

We can create an orthographic projection in D3 using the `d3.geo.orthographic()` function.

Albers projection

Albers projection maps the sphere onto a cone with equal area where the parallels are more closely spaced, and the north and south end and the meridians are equally spaced. This projection is often used to display the areas of geographic features on the map regions with a large east-west distance; in other words, it is commonly used for the Choropleth maps of the US:

The Albers projection

In D3, we can create an Albers projection by the following function:

```
var projection = d3.geo.conicEqualArea();
```

To adapt the projection to the region of interest, we can specify the projection's Albert standard parallels with the `projection.parallels([parallels])` method. The argument called `parallels` should be an array of two latitude values in degree that define the lower and upper bound of the region of interest; for the US, this would be `[29.5, 45.5]`. D3 also offers the `d3.geo.albers()` projection, which is an Albers projection with presets for the US.

At the top, D3 provides another US specific preset, the `d3.geo.albersUsa()` projection, which is displayed in the following figure. We can see that, in addition to the normal US-centric projection, it shows Alaska and Hawaii and hence all the 50 states of the US. Note that the size of Alaska is scaled by a factor of 0.35 in order to fit in the map:

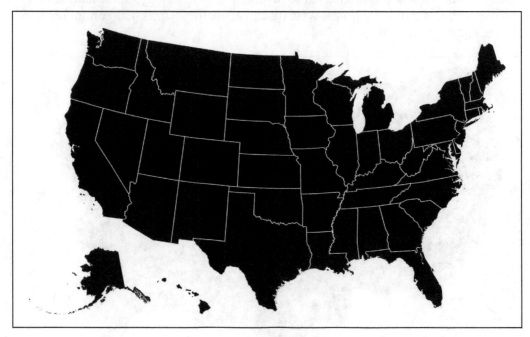

An Albers USA projection

Spherical Mercator projection

The Mercator projection preserves angles locally, which has the nice property that the relative angles on each point of the map are correct; and even the local scale stays constant in any direction. However, as we can see in the following figure, it introduces big distortions on the world scale:

The Mercator projection

Due to its local properties, the Mercator projection is often used by tiled mapping libraries, such as Google Maps and Leaflet. However, it should not be used for Choropleth maps due to the length distortions.

In D3, we create a Mercator projection by calling the `d3.geo.mercator()` function.

Azimuthal Equidistant projection

Azimuthal Equidistant projection maps circles around the projection's center to circles in the 2D map, thus preserving distances in the azimuthal direction from the projection's center:

The Azimuthal Equidistant projection

The projection can be generated by calling the `d3.geo.azimuthalEquidistant()` function. It can be quite useful in a visualization where you want to display distances relative to a certain reference point.

 You can find many more projections and detailed information on Github at `https://github.com/mbostock/d3/wiki/Geo-Projections`.

Helpful tools for creating maps in D3

Drawing maps requires a combination of knowledge and good understanding of GIS, GeoJSON, Projections, and so on as well as techniques and skills for creating the maps. In this section, we will look at a few selected tools that facilitate the generation of interactive maps with D3.

Color scales

As we discussed in the first section, the colors and color scales that the author chooses can have a huge impact for the reader to perceive the visualization. Therefore, I want to show how we can efficiently create color scales in D3.

Scales can map a certain domain of values to a range of different values using interpolation. We usually use this to create scales for axes. Axes, however, map a domain of values onto a pixel range. In our case, we want to use these scales on colors to map a value domain to a color range. We can achieve this using these color interpolation functions:

- d3.interpolateRgb: RGB and HEX values, such as #00FF00
- d3.interpolateHsl: HSL values, such as hsl(120, 100%, 50%)
- d3.interpolateLab: LAB values
- d3.interpolateHcl: HCL values

Let's look at a simple example where we map the values of a domain from 0 to 5 onto a color range from orange to red:

```
var color = d3.scale.linear()
  .interpolate(d3.interpolateRgb)
  .domain([0, 5])
  .range(['#FFCC66', '#FF0000']);

color(0); // > '#FFCC66'
color(5); // > '#FF0000'
```

In the preceding code, we can simply use the d3.interpolateRgb interpolation function to use scales for colors.

Instead of linear scales, we can also use other scales such as the d3.scale.log() logarithmic scale or the d3.scale.pow() exponential scale. If you deal with ordinal values, you can also use non-numeric ordinal scales:

```
var color = d3.scale.ordinal()
  .domain(['foo', 'bar', 'baz'])
  .range(['red', 'blue', 'green']);
```

In the preceding code, we can only map the precise values called foo, bar, and baz to the predefined colors. If you want to use predefined color classes with CSS, you should look into quantized scales, such as d3.scale.quantize() and d3.scale.threshold().

If you are interested in creating beautiful color scales, you should take a look at the *Color Brewer* library at `http://colorbrewer2.org/`.

If you want to display the color scale next to the visualization, you can use the great d3 color legend plugin by John Goodall at `https://github.com/jgoodall/d3-colorlegend`.

The geographic shape generator

You have already learned about the different types that are supported in the GeoJSON format, each one defines a specific geometry. When dealing with these GeoJSON features, we often have the problem of drawing these shapes onto a map using a certain predefined projection. However, I should send flowers to Mike Bostock for developing the geographic shape generator which can be accessed via `d3.geo.path()`.

The D3 geographic shape generator makes it trivial to plot GeoJSON features on a map. It can draw any of the supported GeoJSON types and output the geometry according to a predefined projection as a string for SVG path elements.

Let's take a look at how to use this generator:

```
var projection = d3.geo.albersUsa();
var path = d3.geo.path()
  whitespace ".projection(projection)"

svg.append("path")
    .datum({type: "FeatureCollection", features: features})
    .attr("d", path);
```

In the preceding code, we generated a path for a `FeatureCollection` object with a fictive array of feature. Note that this is the exact GeoJSON format that makes it super simple to plot GeoJSON features.

Graticule – grids on maps

An essential tool to understand maps and projections is a grid in cartographic visualizations. Grids are essential because other than in Cartesian coordinate systems, grids of parallels and meridians are no longer equally spaced or normal onto each other. Hence, the graticule carries a lot of useful visualization about the current projection and geographic coordinate system.

Let's take a look on how to create such a graticule. D3 provides the `d3.geo.graticule()` function that generates a grid for a geographic coordinate system. All we have to do is to plug it into the geo shape generator and style it a little:

```
var width = 960
    height = 960;

var projection = d3.geo.orthographic()
  .scale(width*0.25)
  .translate([width / 2, height / 2])
  .clipAngle(90)
  .precision(.1);
var path = d3.geo.path()
  .projection(projection);
var graticule = d3.geo.graticule();
var svg = d3.select("body").append("svg")
  .attr("width", width)
  .attr("height", height);
svg.append("path")
  .datum(graticule)
  .attr("class", "graticule")
  .attr("d", path);
```

In the preceding code, we create an orthographic projection and plug it into the geo path generator. Finally, we create a graticule and apply it onto the generator. The resulting grid is displayed in the following figure:

A Graticule of the Orthographic projection

Loading multiple resources

As you have already learned in the previous section, we always have to load the geometry of the background map in addition to the file containing the data that we want to display. This is a little challenging because now we have to wait until these (at least) two files have loaded before we can draw the visualization.

Ideally, we want to load both resources in parallel and execute a callback function once all the resources are available. Luckily, Mike Bostock was very active in the past years and wrote the utility tool `Queue.js` which does exactly this.

You can install `Queue.js` using bower and run the following command from the command line or load `Queue.js` from a CDN:

```
bower install queue-async
```

Now, we can create a queue and use the `.defer()` function to register functions to load all the resources. We pass a function as the first argument, and `Queue.js` will automatically pass all additional arguments to this function. Finally, we call the `.await()` method to execute a callback once all the resources have loaded and collect all their values. Let's look at an example:

```
queue()
  .defer(d3.text, "path/to/file/file1.txt")
  .defer(d3.json, "path/to/file/file2.json")
  .defer(d3.csv, "path/to/file/file3.csv")
  .await(function(err, file1, file2, file3) {
    console.log(file1, file2, file3);
  });
```

In the preceding code, we see how easy it is now to deal with multiple resources at once—super easy, thanks to Mike Bostock.

 More information about `Queue.js` can be found on the Github page of the project at `https://github.com/mbostock/queue`.

Types of geographic visualization

According to the values and quantities that we want to display, we can choose from various visualizations that can best represent the data. Usually, we choose between line charts, bar charts, area charts (normal or stacked), pie charts, scatter plots, and so on.

It is easy to understand that the same is true for cartographic visualizations. Besides choosing the type of projection that can represent our data properly, we can also choose between the different types of visualization. This section gives an overview of the most common types of cartographic visualization.

Okay, I have talked enough about the theory — let's draw some maps!

Symbol maps

Our first map will be a simple symbol map as the one in the following figure. We want to display all earthquakes from the US recorded during the last 30 days; the dataset is taken from `http://earthquake.usgs.gov/`:

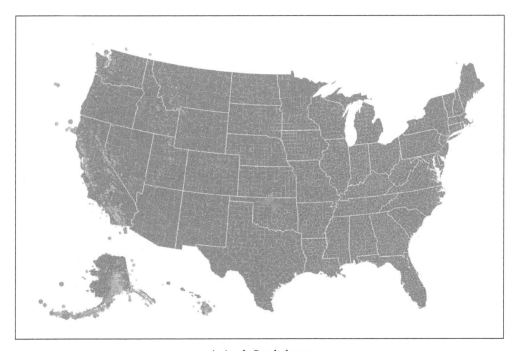

A simple Symbol map

As we can see in the preceding figure, we want to display differently sized and colored points for each earthquake according to its magnitude. Let's start and set up a simple template with d3, TopoJSON, `Queue.js`, and a simple responsive SVG container:

```
<!doctype HTML>
<html>
  <head>
    <script src="bower_components/d3/d3.min.js"></script>
```

```
      <script src="bower_components/topojson/topojson.js"></script>
      <script src="bower_components/queue-async/queue.min.js"></script>
      <style></style>
    </head>
    <body>

    <script>

      var padding = 10,
          body = d3.select("body"),
          width = body.node().clientWidth - padding,
          aspectRatio = 16.0 / 9.0,
          height = width / aspectRatio;

      var svg = d3.select("body").append("svg")
        .attr("width", width)
        .attr("height", height);

      // The visualization code goes here
    </script>
    </body>
</html>
```

In the preceding code, we get the size of the browser window using the `clientWidth` property and define an aspect ratio of 16/9 for the map. We will also use this setting for the other examples.

First, we need to create a projection and draw the map; we will translate and scale the projection to show the map on the full width of the container (note that the scale is interpreted differently in different projections):

```
var projection = d3.geo.albersUsa()
  .scale(width)
  .translate([width / 2, height / 2]);
```

Next, we can also create the path generator using the projection:

```
var path = d3.geo.path()
  .projection(projection);
```

Let's use a simple linear color scale from orange to red values:

```
var color = d3.scale.linear()
  .interpolate(d3.interpolateRgb)
  .domain([0.1, 5])
  .range(['#FFCC66', '#FF0000']);
```

Great, let's load the map and the data and then draw the map. To do so, we will use the TopoJSON format of the US map provided by Mike Bostock at `https://gist.github.com/mbostock/4090848`:

```
queue()
  .defer(d3.json, "data/us.json")
  .defer(d3.json, "data/earthquakes.json")
  .await(ready);
```

Once the resources are available, the `ready` function gets called. Let's implement it:

```
function ready(error, us, earthquakes) {
  if (error) throw error;

  svg.append("g")
      .attr("class", "counties")
    .selectAll("path")
      .data(topojson.feature(us, us.objects.counties).features)
    .enter().append("path")
      .attr("d", path);

  svg.append("path")
      .datum(topojson.mesh(us, us.objects.states))
      .attr("class", "states")
      .attr("d", path);
}
```

In the preceding code, all the data of the deferred functions gets passed as arguments in the order of calling the functions. The US map is stored in TopoJSON format. Therefore, we need to transform it back to valid GeoJSON. We do this using either the `topojson.feature()` or `topojson.mesh()` function. First, we will draw a path for every county in the `us.objects.counties` collection. Next, we will draw one single mesh for all states in the `us.objects.states` collection.

Finally, we are only missing the dots; let's draw them:

```
svg.append("g")
  .attr("class", "data")
    .selectAll('circle')
      .data(earthquakes.features)
      .enter().append('circle')
      .attr('r', function(d){
        return Math.abs(d.properties.mag);
      })
      .attr('fill', function(d){
        return color(Math.abs(d.properties.mag));
```

```
    })
    .attr('transform', function(d) {
        var pos = projection([d.geometry.coordinates[0], d.geometry.
coordinates[1]]);
        if (pos) {
            return "translate(" + pos + ")";
        }
    });
```

The earthquake data is formatted as GeoJSON and available in the `earthquake.`
`features` object. We draw one circle for each element in the collection and adapt the
radius size and color of the shape. Finally, we do some error checking and translate
the circle shape into its proper position on the map. We use the projection function to
achieve this. That's it, the final result is displayed in the previous figure.

Choropleth maps

In the next map, we want to display unemployment rates per county in the US; the
dataset shows unemployment rates per county ordered by county id, taken from
Mike Bostock at `https://gist.github.com/mbostock/4060606`. The result of the
map is shown in the following figure:

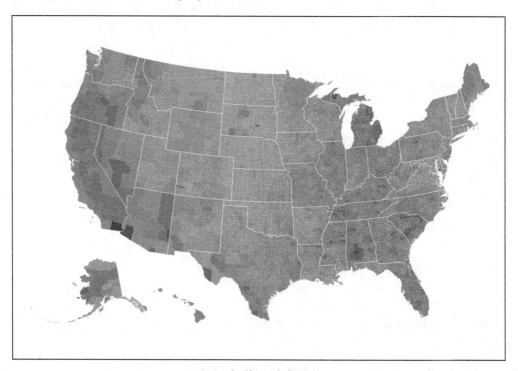

A simple Choropleth map

We can see in the previous figure that we want to color each county according to its unemployment rate. We use the same template (same dimensions and projection) as in the previous example.

Let's create a color scale and load the map and the data; this step is quite similar to the previous example:

```
var color = d3.scale.linear()
  .domain([0, .15])
  .interpolate(d3.interpolateRgb)
  .range(["#FF7948","#B93200"]);
queue()
  .defer(d3.json, "data/us.json")
  .defer(d3.csv, "data/unemployment.csv")
  .await(ready);
```

Now, we can draw the map:

```
function ready(error, us, unemployment) {
  if (error) throw error;
  var data = {};
  unemployment.forEach(function(d){
    data[d.id] = +d.rate;
  });
  svg.append("g")
      .attr("class", "counties")
    .selectAll("path")
      .data(topojson.feature(us, us.objects.counties).features)
    .enter().append("path")
      .attr("fill", function(d) { return color(data[d.id]); })
      .attr("d", path);

  svg.append("path")
      .datum(topojson.mesh(us, us.objects.states))
      .attr("class", "states")
      .attr("d", path);
}
```

In the preceding code, we first transform the unemployment array into an object that stores the unemployment according to the county ID as properties. Then, we draw the counties and fill in the color according to the unemployment rate.

Summary

In this chapter, you learned all the necessities to draw cartographic visualizations with D3. You learned about the geographic coordinate system, the graticules, and color scales.

GeoJSON is an important format to encode geometric features; it can store different types of geometries and values. However, it also stores a lot of redundant information; that's where TopoJSON comes handy.

Finally, we start drawing different cartographic visualizations, such as symbol maps and Choropleth maps.

In the next chapter, you will learn about testing the responsive visualizations.

8
Testing Responsive Visualizations

In the previous chapter, you learned how to create amazing cartographic visualizations using D3.js, projections, and geographic maps. Now, it is time to look into the testing strategies of responsive visualizations. In this section, you will learn the following:

- Learning about common testing strategies
- Understanding the difference of unit and integration tests
- Learning about the importance of manual tests in visualizations
- Learning how to set up an environment for manual testing
- Setting up an environment for Unit and Integration testing
- Running unit tests using Karma on your local machine
- Running integration tests using TravisCI and Sauce Labs using a testing environment
- Understanding how the different strategies work together
- Building a testing strategy that fits your budget

In the first section, you will learn about testing, testing strategies, and different types of tests. You will understand the differences between manual and automated testing and why it is crucial to have great tools in your workflow for manual testing.

In the next section, we will take a closer look at these manual testing and debugging tools. We will find out how to use **Browsersync**, **Browserstack**, Device Modes, and much more to boost up your local development environment.

Then, we will discuss automated tests, an important part of writing maintainable code. We will not only look into some local unit testing with Karma but also integration testing using Protractor, Selenium, Travis CI, and Sauce Labs.

Finally, we will summarize how a great development environment should look when you care about testing and code quality.

A guide on testing visualizations

At the end of this chapter, you will have a clear idea about testing strategies for responsive visualizations; you will be aware about the costs and benefits of testing; and you will be able to implement both manual and automated tests with the best tools that are available today.

If you are new to software development, you may have heard about testing and testing strategies and how many developers pretend that they are obsessed about testing. However, it is very important to understand the differences between, for example, test-driven development in software development and manual testing and debugging, in order to compare the costs and benefits for these strategies. If you are already writing tests on a daily basis and have a clear strategy about unit and integration tests, you might skip this introduction and jump directly to the next section. For everyone else, I promise that you will learn some great insights and information about testing, so go ahead!

When testing interactive visualizations, we are somehow in a very difficult domain. On the one hand, we write code, so we need to make sure that all functions of the code do exactly what they should. However, on the other hand, we produce visualizations that should look and feel the same across all different devices, operating systems, and browsers—something that can only be evaluated manually. The goal is to combine the best of manual testing and automated tools to maximize productivity and maintainability and minimize the number of errors in the code.

 In this chapter, I will mention tools and services that may require a paid subscription. My intention is not to sell you a subscription to one of these services but to present the best tools for manual and automated cross-browser testing from my experience.

Why should I care about testing?

Testing your code is crucial to write a great bug-free and maintainable software. However, writing a ton of automated tests too early can slow down development and affect productivity. Therefore, we need to find a good trade-off between writing code, debugging, and testing.

Tests greatly improve the maintainability of your code. Unit tests, for example, can serve as a documentation for developers which on top can also be executed. Whenever a developer modifies the code or refactors it, he/she can always run the tests to see if a function still works as expected. This makes the code much easier and safer to refactor. Therefore, writing tests is crucial to build maintainable software and saves time and costs while maintaining an application.

The goal of a test is to assure that a function works as expected after re-factorings and modifications. Hence, your tests should cover a combination of all the possible input arguments and test all the possible output values. By writing good tests, you can be quite sure that your application works properly. However, keep in mind the following things:

- Tests can never prove the absence of bugs; it can rather guarantee that for the given test cases, the software performs as expected

- Bugs can also occur if your software is very well tested and all your tests pass

- Tests are usually performed in a testing environment; make sure that your test environment is as similar as possible to your production environment, especially for integration and system tests

I want to emphasize that developers should focus on test quality rather than quantity. Test quality cannot be measured, whereas the quantity can, by computing how many lines of code have actually been executed—this is called the test coverage If the tests have executed every single `if` condition, iterated over every `for` loop, and reached every `return` statement, then the test coverage is 100%. This leads to the misconception that a high test coverage (optimally 100%) is the most important goal.

However, keep in mind that 100% test coverage doesn't guarantee bug-free code. Actually, it just means that 100% of your code has been executed. It doesn't even tell us anything about the quality of the tests. 80% to 90% test coverage with meaningful and good tests should be preferred as a good trade-off.

One might ask what a good test looks like compared to a bad one. A good test is one that finds a bug or unexpected behavior (these two things are actually the same). A good test tries to break the software, discover the unexpected behavior, and tests all the possible edge cases for the input arguments. The person writing the tests should not be gentle and kind to the software but preferably try to break it because the purpose of tests is to break the software. A bad test tests the behavior of the software only for arguments in its typical range and expected output.

The different types of test

I've already confused you by speaking about different strategies, so let's get clear about them and take a look at different testing strategies.

Manual tests

When I speak about *manual testing*, I mean opening the application on your laptop or mobile phone and clicking around in it.

If we are in the domain of software development, manual tests are a no go. You would never rely on manual tests and always prefer automated tests as they are more reliable, reproducible, and much faster than manual ones.

However, in UX/UI design and graphics, manual tests are the only reliable way of finding errors fast—but why is this? This is because when dealing with graphics, humans are much better to spot visual errors or lags of interactive elements. It would be much more tedious and time consuming to write automated tests from the very beginning of every visualization, transition, or animation. Therefore, when dealing with responsive design or graphics, testing your visualizations manually is a necessary step in the development pipeline. Manual tests help to identify errors quickly and be productive.

The easiest way to test a responsive application manually would be setting up two Chrome windows—one for testing the desktop version and one for testing the mobile version (with the mobile device mode enabled). You will always have to test your application in each window and reload your application on changes.

One could enhance the setup by adding an Android, iOS, or Windows Phone emulator to the local development system; one would even test the application on some real hardware maybe. To optimize the manual testing workflow, add a live-reload or browser sync feature to all your devices to avoid manual reloading on all the devices. You can also add remote devices from a remote device farm in the cloud to your local setup so that your application runs on some real hardware and gets controlled through the browser. The section about *Manual Testing* will help you in setting up such an environment step by step and discuss all the preceding options in detail.

Automated tests

When I speak about automated testing, I mean a test script that runs a number of tests without manual interaction. The result of the automated tests is either pass (green) or fail (red) when either *all tests passed* or *one (or more) tests failed*. Ideally, one would run this script after making changes to the local files to quickly discover functional bugs. If the test script is slow, one could also run it automatically after committing changes to the code repository.

In the domain of software development, automated tests are always the preferred way of testing, as it is a reliable and repeatable way of testing code. Usually, we differentiate three strategies for automated testing:

- **Unit tests**: Testing single units (functions), often called specifications (specs)
- **Integration tests**: testing the integration of units (multiple functions), often called end-to-end (e2e) testing
- **System tests**: testing the whole system

We can conclude that every strategy should be applied in a different stage and under different constraints due to the complexity of the test setup and the runtimes of the tests. While unit tests are, in general, very fast, they can be run locally on every change of the source files. Integration and system tests are typically slow and should run in a remote testing environment, for example, after every commit to the source code repository.

There are many components in visualizations that can be tested in an automated way, such as scales, mapping functions, reducers, the drawing of elements, and more, both on the local system and a remote testing environment. Hence, I will introduce you to the world of unit and integration testing in the section *Automated Testing*, and we will implement a typical automated testing strategy for visual components.

In this book, we only deal with visualization components; and therefore, we will only look into unit and integration tests. They are described in the following sections.

Semi-automated tests

Some tests are executed automatically; but determining whether they've passed or failed can't be done by a program. What sounds a little bit scary at first can be better described with an example.

Let's think about a simple cartographic visualization. You add a graticule to the visualization to make it easier for the user to perceive distances in the map. Your test script is generating a screenshot of your application, and compares it to the one from the previous version; to be more precise, it computes the absolute difference between the two screenshots. This technique is called **Visual Regression Testing**.

How can the script decide whether the grid has been added intentionally or it is a bug that occurs from a change in the code? It simply cannot do so. The script runs automatically; however, it requires a human interaction to pass the test; this is what we call a semi-automated test. Sometimes, (small) visual changes are made intentionally, and sometimes, they can be produced by bugs. It is impossible to automatically decide which change is intended.

In a good data visualization setup, we would generate a set of screenshots and provide pictures with the absolute difference from the previous version to the developer whenever he/she commits a change to the source code repository. To facilitate focusing on the most important changes, the script can only show images to the developer that has changed more than a certain threshold of pixels.

Unit tests

Unit tests (or specs) aim to test the smallest units of your code for correctness; and hence, they provide an executable documentation of all the units of your code. While it is debatable what the smallest unit of your code is, in my opinion the smallest unit is a single function.

In data visualizations, it is a good technique to use a functional approach to design your components in such a way that every function receives an input, modifies it, and returns an output. A good strategy would be to write tests for all these functions.

Units test should only affect the code from the tested unit and not require any other units, so everything besides the tested unit should be mocked. Mocks are the copies of objects created specifically for testing that (synchronously) return a predefined result. Let's think about `XMLHttpRequest` in one of our functions. We can simply create a Mock that synchronously returns a predefined result for this request. The benefit is clear. It is much faster as we don't have to create a real request. It's also repeatable and doesn't depend on the real result of the XHR.

This brings us to the second most important statement about unit tests: they should run locally after each change in the source code and therefore be super-fast. Thus, we most often run the unit tests in a headless browser (without the graphics), such as **PhantomJS**, on our local development environment.

Integration tests

Integration tests (or e2e) aim to test the integration of components from the position of a user interacting with the component. This means that they test the interplay of multiple components in a real browser for user interactions.

A good strategy for data visualizations would be the testing of each interaction possibility, such as drawing, clicking, hover, zooming, filtering, and so on. In comparison to unit tests, we need a real browser (with mouse, touch, scrolling, and more) and multiple components for integrating tests. Hence, the test suite will run much slower than the one for unit tests.

A good workflow is to run the integration test before you commit a change to your repository on your local development environment and every time you push changes to your repository in the development environment.

Continuous Integration

If you have a setup where a change on the repository trigger tests in a testing environment, we speak of a so-called *Continuous Integration*. If you have ever worked with code on Github, you must have certainly noticed these tiny Build passing badges on some repository Readme files. This is very likely the status file of the build/test status from a service called **TravisCI** which can be tightly integrated with Github. However, there are also other services that provide similar functionality and badges.

Besides TravisCI, there exists another great service for continuous integration that is called **Codeship**. It gives you many more options for your testing environment, and you can even run your tests in parallel.

A good setup for a data visualization always uses Continuous Integration. It is super easy to set it up, and you can immediately see the test status of all your branches.

Test-driven development (TDD)

During the last decade, TDD has become very popular among software engineers. It's a technique where you first implement your tests before writing the actual code. The goal of this method is to think about the purpose of your function before you implement it.

TDD greatly improves the quality of your code because developers are forced to think about the exact purpose of each function before implementing it. This works great for good developers when writing components with clearly defined scope and purpose.

However, in data visualizations, most of the work is done iteratively and by exploration; we add axis, scales, colors, play around with dimensions, move the legend, and so on. It's more like programmatically designing a graphic with code. I claim that it is contra-productive to use TDD for visualizations because you will waste a lot of time rewriting tests while experimenting with your visualization.

Manual testing and debugging

Let's start with manual testing, debugging your responsive application locally on your development machine. For this purpose, I created a little dashboard application that is displayed in the following screenshot. The picture is a screenshot from a Chrome window on my desktop computer:

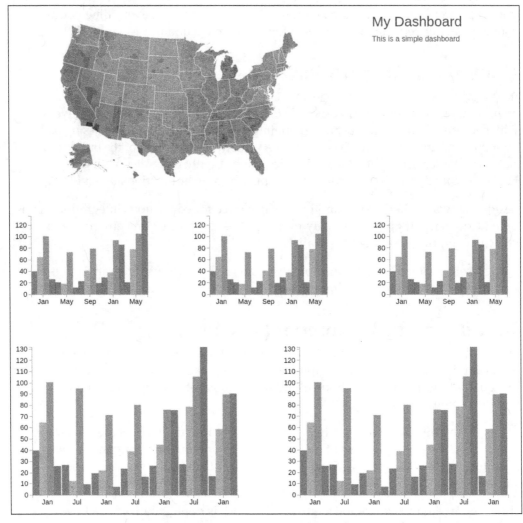

The dashboard application with visualization components

Testing and debugging locally

Running your devices locally has one big benefit: it is super fast, and you can quickly see how the visualization feels. You have control over the device; it's either in your hands or running on your local machine. The following figure shows a typical local development setup:

The local development setup

Changing Device Modes in a Chrome desktop browser

The fastest and most convenient way of quickly testing an application with a different screen resolution is to use the Device Mode setting in the Chrome Developer Tools. You can open it by first opening the Developer Tools (pressing *F12*) and then clicking on the tiny mobile phone icon on the top left-hand side. In the following figure, you can see the Developer Tools with a little mobile phone in blue, which means that Device Mode is enabled:

```
Elements    Console    Sources    Network    »                    ⋮    ✕
<!DOCTYPE html>
<html>
▶ #shadow-root (open)
▶ <head>…</head>
▼ <body>
   ▶ <script type="text/javascript" id="__bs_script__">…</script>
     <script async src="/browser-sync/browser-sync-
     client.2.11.1.js"></script>
   ▶ <div class="container">…</div>
     <script>

            barchart('.barchart');
            choropleth('.choropleth');

     </script>
   ▶ <div id="window-resizer-tooltip">…</div>
   </body>
</html>
```

```
html  body
```

Developer Tools in Chrome

Once we activate Device Mode, the background of the browser window turns into a gray-colored grid and only shows the frame in the typical resolution of a mobile device. In the following screenshot, we can see the active Device Mode for the presets of an iPad:

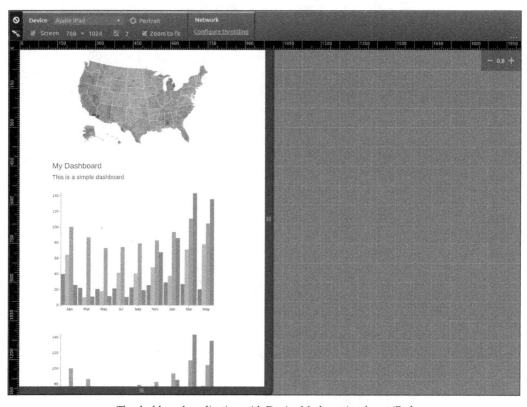

The dashboard application with Device Mode setting for an iPad

One can easily understand why this type of testing is very elegant; it is very fast, we can stay in our local environment and use all the debugging tools that we have always used. However, we should be aware that Device Mode only adapts the window to fit the screen size and resolution of the target device but does not emulate the browser. Therefore, Device Mode enables us to only test different screen resolutions and not the cross-browser compatibility.

> You can find more information about Device Mode on the Chrome Developer website at `https://developer.` `chrome.com/devtools/docs/device-mode`.

Emulating mobile devices

In the next step, we can argue that we not only want to emulate the browser screen of the target device, we also emulate the device on its own and use device emulators. Those who already develop software for Android or iOS might have their official emulator installed. Emulating on a system level leads to much more accurate results when testing cross-browser compatibility because of the emulation of the systems architecture running the real mobile browser of the target system.

However, there are some drawbacks of working with emulators. Most importantly, there is currently no way to install Android, iOS, and Windows emulators on the same operating system without using virtual machines or dual boot; and second, working with emulators is horribly slow. To be honest, I haven't tested the latest versions of the official emulators; but the last time I used them, it was simply too slow to work on a daily basis.

Starting up the emulator takes a lot of time, and running them takes too many resources of the host PC. However, if your target platform is, for example, Android, and you already have an Android environment installed, it might be a good way to go.

 You can find more resources about the Android emulator on the Android website at `http://tools.android.com/tech-docs/emulator`. If you use Android and are looking for a faster emulator, you should take a look at Genymotion at `https://www.genymotion.com`.

Syncing Real Devices using Browsersync

I prefer to test my code on real devices, which I have lying around in my office: three Android phones, one Android tablet, and one Windows phone. The Android phones all have different major versions of Android installed.

Opening the same visualization on all these devices and testing them is a pain. It would take too much time. Thankfully, there is an amazing tool called Browsersync that lets you sync your current page to all the connected devices, push URLs, auto-reload pages, and mirror clicks and scrolling. I really don't know how developers could ever be productive without a tool like this.

It has to be installed only on your host computer, which is your local development Desktop machine, by running the following code from the command line:

```
npm install -g browser-sync
```

This installs the tool and makes the `browser-sync` command globally available. By running the following command, you start a development server that serves all the static files from your directory and monitors all JavaScript files for changes:

```
browser-sync start --server --files "*.js"
```

When a change occurs, Browsersync pushes these changes to all connected clients via **WebSockets** and hot reload. It works on all mobile devices with a web browser, even on my old Windows Phone.

When running the `start` command, Browsersync shows you two different domains: one to connect to the development server and another to the Browsersync UI. Connecting to the host is as easy as opening this URL with the mobile devices. The following screenshot shows the dashboard application opened with an Android phone:

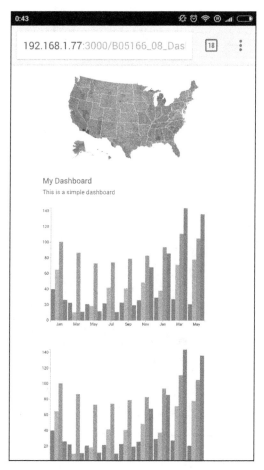

The dashboard application on an Android phone

You actually cannot see it on the picture, but by scrolling in the application also all connected devices scroll to the same position. The following screenshot shows the same application on an Android tablet:

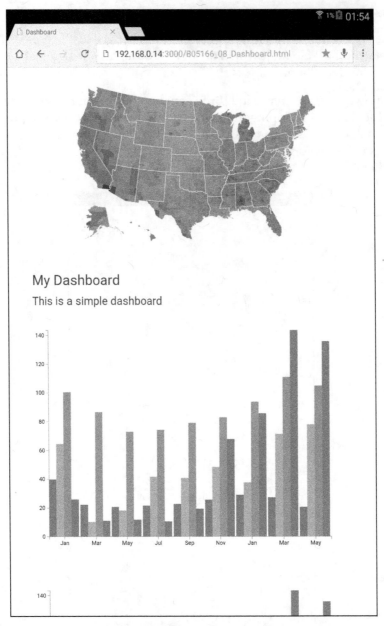

The dashboard application on an Android tablet

If you have a few spare target devices, then using Browsersync is a really convenient way to quickly test your visualization on real devices.

 You can find more information about Browsersync on the `https://www.browsersync.io/` website.

Remote-debugging responsive applications

If you can't afford real devices and don't fancy running emulators on your local machine, you can also decide to access all the devices you want from a device lab in the cloud. This combines fast access with small costs and a great variety of different device types:

The Device Lab in the cloud (source: Browserstack)

If you are testing web applications, you should probably try the browser device lab **Browserstack**. It gives you access to a magnitude of different browsers and devices all from within your browser. It's a little bit expensive to run your tests in the *Automate* mode but great to use in the so-called *live* mode. This lets you run and control a browser on the device through your local browser (see the following screenshot showing Safari running on a Mac controlled through Ubuntu).

In combination with the previously discussed Browsersync, you can also open a local URL with the browser instances of Safari running on a Mac as shown in the following figure. Keep in mind that opening local URLs requires an extra browser plugin to tunnel the traffic through your local network. However, this gives you the exact same features as we saw before: URL pushing, click mirroring, auto-reload, and so on. It is a deadly combination with a huge variety of remote devices, operating systems, and browsers.

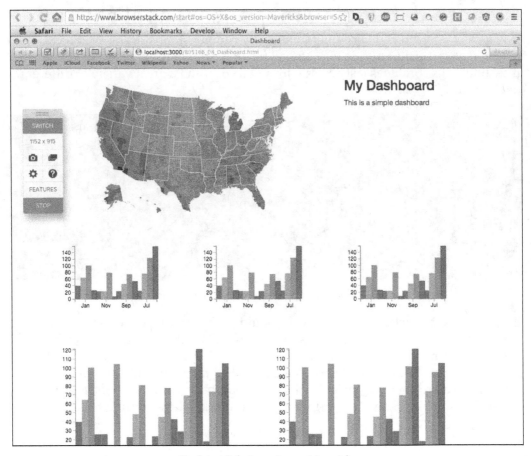

The latest Safari running on Mavericks

In the next screenshot, you can see the iOS browser of iOS running on an iPhone 6 Plus that is again controlled via a Chromium browser running on Ubuntu. It's unbelievable easy to test and debug on different devices. You can even open Developer Tools on the remote devices. This is especially handy on mobile devices where you would usually not be able to open the Developer Tools and debug the application that easily.

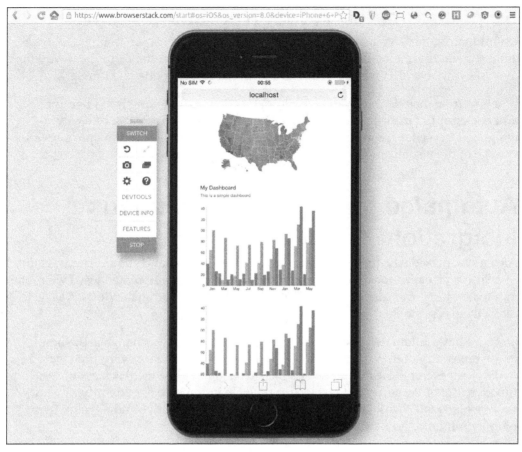

The latest Safari running on iPhone 6 Plus

Testing and debugging on Browserstack is not cheap, but it is a great benefit for every developer. Having a direct and immediate access to the magnitude of different browsers and devices is incredible. The fact that you can tunnel it through your local network and access your local development server is simply amazing.

 You can find more information about Browserstack and local testing on the Browserstack website at `https://www.browserstack.com/local-testing`.

Semi-automated visual Regression tests

Unfortunately, there are no common strategies for visual regression testing due to the ambiguity and customizability of the tests and the results. To establish a great workflow that uses Github and TravisCI it requires a bit of manual scripting and tuning.

If you want to include it in your workflow, I recommend looking into PhantomCSS and **BackstopJS** (an abstraction on top of Phantom). These tools can be easily integrated into your testing strategy to create regression images from your previous version of the visualization.

Automated testing and Continuous Integration

As we saw previously, there are many cases where we can and should run tests for responsive visualizations. In any case where we can write automated tests, we prefer automated tests over manual tests. The reason we prefer automated tests is easy: to make them repeatable.

Once we have automated tests, we can run them every time a change is pushed to the repository. If they are fast enough, we can even run them every time we make changes to the local source files. This gives immediate feedback about the functionality of the code, and fast feedback. Debugging is easier, identifying and finding bugs, which automatically makes you more productive and development more effective.

Running tests on your local machine

Finally, we can start to write some tests and run them automatically. We will start with unit tests and speak about integration tests afterward.

Running unit tests using Karma

As a first tool to write and run unit tests, we need a tool that can collect all the tests, set up the testing environment, and start the tests in a web browser instance. These are the tasks of the so-called test runner. In this book, we will use the Karma test runner, which was developed by the Angular team.

Karma is very easy to configure and use, and it integrates nicely into your Gulp and Grunt build configurations. It can be installed via the following command:

```
npm install karma -save-dev
```

This command also adds Karma to the current development dependencies. Once Karma is installed, you can set up a configuration using this command:

```
karma init karma.conf.js
```

In this book, I selected the test framework called Mocha, `Require.js` and the browser called PhantomJS to run the tests; you will receive an output similar to the following figure:

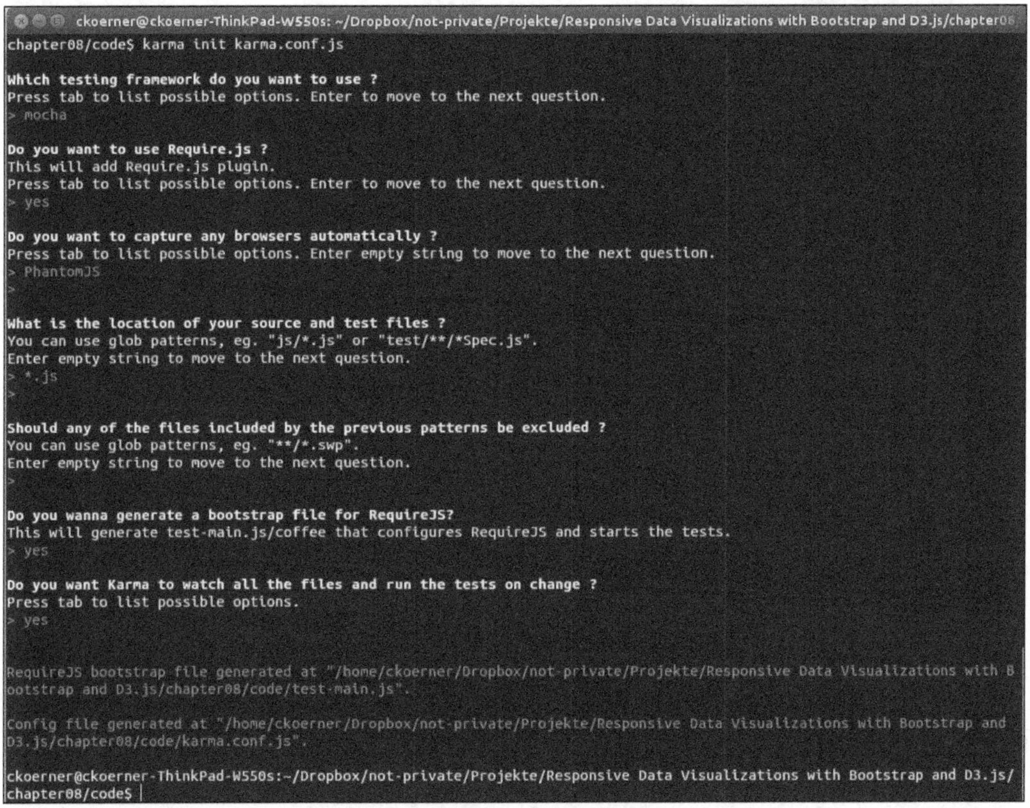

Installing and configuring Karma

Make sure you have Mocha, Chai, `Require.js`, and PhantomJS installed by running the following command:

```
npm install phantomjs mocha chai karma-chai requirejs -save-dev
```

Finally, we can add `chai` and `app.js` to our JavaScript code to the configuration (you can take a look in the source code) and start Karma by running the following from the command line:

```
karma start
```

If we have configured Karma properly, it will start up a PhantomJS instance and run all tests. However, if we don't have any tests yet, we will get an error such as `int` the following figure. Great, now is the time to write our first unit test:

```
ckoerner@ckoerner-ThinkPad-W550s: ~/Dropbox/not-private/Projekte/Responsive Data Visualizations with Bootstrap and D3.js/chapter08
ckoerner@ckoerner-ThinkPad-W550s:~/Dropbox/not-private/Projekte/Responsive Data Visualizations with Bootstrap and D3.js/
chapter08/code$ karma start
25 01 2016 00:10:05.486:WARN [karma]: No captured browser, open http://localhost:9876/
25 01 2016 00:10:05.495:INFO [karma]: Karma v0.13.19 server started at http://localhost:9876/
25 01 2016 00:10:05.500:INFO [launcher]: Starting browser PhantomJS
25 01 2016 00:10:06.290:INFO [PhantomJS 1.9.8 (Linux 0.0.0)]: Connected on socket /#6jpsD0uFplXgkSl3AAAA with id 4778957
6
PhantomJS 1.9.8 (Linux 0.0.0): Executed 0 of 0 ERROR (0.001 secs / 0 secs)
```

Running Karma

We have a nice little function that can flatten a nested array for us. This is a perfect example for a unit test called `app.spec.js`; let's write a simple test:

```
var expect = chai.expect;

describe('app', function() {
  describe('#flatten()', function () {

    it('should flatten an nested array', function () {
      var nestedArray = [['foo'], ['bar']];

      var computed = flatten(nestedArray);
      var expected = ['foo', 'bar'];

      expect(computed).to.eql(expected);
    });
  });
});
```

In the preceding code, we wrap all our tests for the component in the `describe` block. Inside this block, we wrap all the tests for the flatten function in the `describe` block. Finally, we write the first test to test against a standard case.

There are many ways and `assertion` libraries to write good and expressive tests; however, I find it very useful to reduce all the tests to the absolute minimum. First, we start with an initialization phase for the `nestedArray` variable. Next, we move to the transform state where we transform the input using the function under test. I always store the output in the `computed` variable. Finally, I declare the expected value using the `expected` variable. Then, I use either `expect(computed).to.eql(expected)` or `expect(computed).to.equal(expected)`. Here, the first one tests element-wise equality and the latter tests the type equality.

As we can see in the following figure, the test passes and Karma shows a green **SUCCESS** status:

```
ckoerner@ckoerner-ThinkPad-W550s: ~/Dropbox/not-private/Projekte/Responsive Data Visualizations with Bootstrap and D3.js/chapter08
ckoerner@ckoerner-ThinkPad-W550s:~/Dropbox/not-private/Projekte/Responsive Data Visualizations with Bootstrap and D3.js/
chapter08/code$ karma start
25 01 2016 00:38:51.176:WARN [karma]: No captured browser, open http://localhost:9876/
25 01 2016 00:38:51.185:INFO [karma]: Karma v0.13.19 server started at http://localhost:9876/
25 01 2016 00:38:51.191:INFO [launcher]: Starting browser PhantomJS
25 01 2016 00:38:52.191:INFO [PhantomJS 1.9.8 (Linux 0.0.0)]: Connected on socket /#_JX9485G8n1Liih2AAAA with id 5513806
2
PhantomJS 1.9.8 (Linux 0.0.0): Executed 1 of 1 SUCCESS (0.003 secs / 0.001 secs)
```

Passing all the tests in Karma

Now would be a good moment to go back to the test and make it fail. What happens if you call the function on an empty array? What if the array is deeply nested? You can already see where this is going; our aim is to break the code.

 More information about the Karma test runner and its configuration can be found on Github at `https://karma-runner.github.io/`. More information about the Mocha test framework can be found on the Mocha Website at `https://mochajs.org/`. If you want to read more about the Chai assertion library, then take a look at `http://chaijs.com/`.

Integration testing using Protractor and Selenium

Integration tests require all the components from the system that are under tests to work as if a user would interacting with the component. Therefore, we need to use a different test runner that can start, stop, and connect to browsers, open URLs, deal with asynchronous code, and extract information about the elements.

In this book, we will also use the Integration testing tool from the AngularJS team: Protractor. It is based on Webdriver and Selenium and therefore very powerful when interacting with different browsers and instances.

We can install Protractor by running the following command from the command line:

```
npm install -g protractor
```

Once Protractor is installed, we have to also install Webdriver. One can do this by running the following:

```
webdriver-manager update
```

To run the integration tests with Protractor, we always have to run Webdriver beforehand. Thus we can start it via:

webdriver-manager start

If you've installed everything properly, you will see an output similar to the following figure:

```
ckoerner@ckoerner-ThinkPad-W550s: ~/Dropbox/not-private/Projekte/Responsive Data Visualizations with Bootstrap and D3.js/chapter08
ckoerner@ckoerner-ThinkPad-W550s:~/Dropbox/not-private/Projekte/Responsive Data Visualizations with Bootstrap and D3.js/
chapter08/code$ webdriver-manager start
seleniumProcess.pid: 21361
01:08:05.260 INFO - Launching a standalone Selenium Server
Setting system property webdriver.chrome.driver to /usr/local/lib/node_modules/protractor/selenium/chromedriver
01:08:05.301 INFO - Java: Oracle Corporation 24.91-b01
01:08:05.302 INFO - OS: Linux 4.2.0-23-generic amd64
01:08:05.316 INFO - v2.48.0, with Core v2.48.0. Built from revision 41bccdd
01:08:05.394 INFO - Driver provider org.openqa.selenium.ie.InternetExplorerDriver registration is skipped:
registration capabilities Capabilities [{platform=WINDOWS, ensureCleanSession=true, browserName=internet explorer, versi
on=}] does not match the current platform LINUX
01:08:05.394 INFO - Driver provider org.openqa.selenium.edge.EdgeDriver registration is skipped:
registration capabilities Capabilities [{platform=WINDOWS, browserName=MicrosoftEdge, version=}] does not match the curr
ent platform LINUX
01:08:05.395 INFO - Driver class not found: com.opera.core.systems.OperaDriver
01:08:05.395 INFO - Driver provider com.opera.core.systems.OperaDriver is not registered
01:08:05.487 INFO - RemoteWebDriver instances should connect to: http://127.0.0.1:4444/wd/hub
01:08:05.487 INFO - Selenium Server is up and running
```

Selenium running in the background

Now, we can create a simple configuration file called `protractor.conf.js` and our first test called `app.e2e.js`. Take a look into the source code for the correct settings:

```
describe('dashboard', function() {
  beforeEach(function() {
    // Don't wait for Angular
    return browser.ignoreSynchronization = true;
  });

  it('load choropleths', function() {
    browser.get('B05166_08_Dashboard.html');

    var maps = element.all(by.css('.choropleth'));

    var result = maps.count();
    var expected = 1;

    expect(result).toEqual(expected);
  });
});
```

In the preceding code, we again wrap all our tests in a describe block. Then, we add a little snippet to tell Protractor not to wait for AngularJS. Finally, we write a tests that accesses the Browsersync development server.

If we start the tests, it runs and hopefully finishes without errors like in the following figure:

Passing all the tests in Protractor

Now would be a good point to create Integration test files that contain a single visual component as well as tests for this component. Try to add scrolling, hovering, and clicking to break the visualization.

> You can find more information about Protractor, its configuration, and API on the Angular website at `https://angular.github.io/protractor`.

Running your tests in the cloud

Now comes the master class; you can write a script to run your complete Integration tests on every push via TravisCI. Take a look at the steps in `https://docs.travis-ci.com/user/languages/javascript-with-nodejs` to get started with Travis and JavaScript.

However, instead of running your browsers in the virtual machine of Travis, you can add a service such as Browserstack to run the tests on multiple devices using multiple resolutions in the cloud.

I want to mention another great Service for automated device testing, which is a great alternative to Browserstack and free for open source projects—Sauce Labs.

> You can find more information about Sauce Labs on their website at `https://saucelabs.com/`.

A testing strategy for visualizations

Now, we have enough information to build a solid testing strategy for responsive visualizations. Note that this is a very opinionated setup based on my experience, and feel free to exchange any layer or tool with your favorite ones. However, keep the general ideas for your workflow.

First, we will use the Chrome browser on the desktop PC while developing. We either use a normal desktop window or we switch to a mobile view in the device mode. This depends on the target screen size and resolution. Personally, I prefer to work in a desktop Chrome and debug and test on mobiles.

While developing, we need to regularly do some manual testing to make sure our visualization looks and feels nice. Running emulators for different operating systems locally is a pain; that's why I prefer syncing a real mobile phone and a tablet via Browsersync to my current Chrome window. If you don't have access to real devices, you can also use Browserstack on your local project.

For unit tests, we need to start a Karma unit runner before we start making changes. This will watch source files for changes, fire up a PhantomJS instance, and run the complete test suite whenever a file is saved.

Once we push a commit to Github, TravisCI automatically runs all unit tests locally and integration tests on different mobile devices using Sauce Lab. This will also create different images for the visual regression test and show them to the developer.

Finally, a feature or fix can be merged into the master when all tests have passed, and the developer accepts the different images of the visual regression.

Summary

This chapter gives a solid overview on different testing strategies for testing responsive visualization components. In the first section, we spoke about the testing strategies, costs, and benefits of testing and the difference between local, remote, manual, and automated tests.

Then, we go through different testing strategies and understand how they can be implemented for the visualization. We cover manual testing using Browsersync and Browserstack, as well as automated testing using TravisCI, Karma, Protractor, and Selenium. Finally, we will build our perfect testing strategy for visualization components.

In the next chapter, you will learn about detecting and solving cross-browser issues when creating responsive visualizations in SVG.

Solving Cross-Browser Issues

In the previous chapter, you learned all about testing the custom responsive visualizations in different browsers. We have to do this because, across different devices, operating systems, and browsers, the appearance and functionality of our application can vary. In this chapter, we will tackle these cross-browser issues. You will learn the following:

- Understanding the main challenges of cross-browser compatible visualizations
- Using Modernizr to detect the feature support of the user's browser
- Learning about Polyfills, Shims, and Wrappers
- Understanding the compatibility of D3
- Implementing a cross-browser responsive design
- Understanding the `matchMedia` polyfill
- Polyfill min-width and max-width with `Respond.js`
- Implementing your Media Queries in JavaScript using `Enquire.js`
- Learning about the compatibility of SVG features
- Understanding compatibility for mouse and touch events
- Understanding the execution chain of touch events
- Building touch-friendly visualizations

First, we will look into general cross-browser compatibility problems and find ways how to solve them. From simple conditional comments for Internet Explorer, we will progress to complex feature detection in JavaScript and CSS using Modernizr. You will understand common concepts to solve cross-browser issues, such as Polyfills, Shims, and Wrappers.

In the second section, you will learn about cross-browser compatible Media Queries and understand the problem of CSS polyfills. Then, we will look into the different solutions of this problem using Respond.js (a min-width max-width polyfill) and Enquire.js, a library to organize your Media Queries in JavaScript.

Next, we will take a look at the support of special SVG features that are not included in the 1.1 specification, such as animations, filters, and the clipping path.

In the last section, you will learn how to handle touch and mouse inputs properly on devices that support both mouse and touch inputs. We will see some common pitfalls, touch events, and how both touch and mouse events can be supported for your application.

A solution to cross-browser compatibility issues

The real challenge of developing web applications is not about implementing awesome features, animations, or transitions, but it is about providing a first-class user experience and compatibility for all target devices, operating systems, and browsers. In this chapter, we will try to solve the most common compatibility issues and make your visualization cross-browser compatible.

Conditional comments for Internet Explorer

A great tool in every web developer's toolbox for solving compatibility issues is conditional comments for HTML. These are the HTML comments that can contain valid HTML code, which are interpreted and executed by Internet Explorer. Wait a second, a cool feature that is only available in Internet Explorer? Well, it turns out that these conditional HTML comments are not necessary in modern web browsers as these browser rather implement the proper standard than proprietary features.

Hence, conditional comments are a great way for the lost souls targeting Internet Explorer to load resources, depending on the browser version. Let's take a look at an easy example where we load a compatibility script only for Internet Explorer with version less than or equal to 9:

```
<!doctype HTML>
<html>
  <head>
    <title>Conditional Comments</title>
    <!--[if lte IE 9]>
    <script src="compatibility_script.js"></script>
    <![ENDIF]-->
```

```
        <script src="some_script.js"></script>
    </head>
    <body>

    </body>
</html>
```

In the preceding example, we can see that `<!--[if lte IE 9]>...<![ENDIF]-->` represents a valid HTML comment that turns into a conditional HTML node in Internet Explorer.

The syntax allows only the `<!--[if ...]>` and `<![ENDIF]-->` keywords and a small variety of expressions, conditions, and operators. The following operators are allowed to identify the browser version:

- `!` not operator, for example, `[if !IE]`
- `lt` less-than operator, for example, `[if lt IE 5.5]`
- `lte` less-than or equal operator, for example, `[if lte IE 6]`
- `gt` greater-than operator, for example, `[if gt IE 5]`
- `gte` greater-than or equal operator, for example, `[if gte IE 7]`
- `( )` subexpression operator, for example, `[if !(IE 7)]`
- `&` and operator, for example, `[if (gt IE 5)&(lt IE 7)]`
- `|` or operator, for example, `[if (IE 6)|(IE 7)]`

 More information about conditional comments in Internet Explorer can be found on MSDN at `https://msdn.microsoft.com/en-us/library/ms537512.aspx`.

Detecting native features with Modernizr

The key challenge of designing responsive applications is to properly adapt the application to the form factor (the screen size and resolution) of the user's device. Knowing the form factor and making use of native tools, such as Media Queries, facilitates creating very responsive applications. Whenever native implementations are available, we want to use them; whenever we can implement something in CSS instead of JavaScript, we want to do so to gain the important performance boost. Hence, if we want to support not just the latest browsers, we need to be able to detect whether a native feature is available or not.

One might ask how a certain feature can be detected on a user's browser. One simple way is to check if an API is available, which is similar to the following example. We check if the native function called `Array.prototype.every` is available:

```
if ('every' in Array.prototype) {
  console.log('Array.prototype.every is available');
}
```

The preceding code can be easily generalized to test against different objects and API functions. However, what if we would like to know if the `in` keyword is available in our browser? Or if arrow functions are supported? This works slightly differently; we have to evaluate the expression in the try-catch block. Here is an example to test whether arrow functions are currently available:

```
function hasArrow() {
  try {
    eval('()=>{}');
  } catch (err) {
    return false;
  }
  return true;
}
```

Using this technique, we can extend this to a magnitude of different features and APIs and check whether these are available or not. However, we are very lazy and don't want to implement all of them. Luckily, there is a wonderful library called Modernizr that does all this for us and additionally provides an easy-to-use, class-based method for feature detection in CSS.

First, we are going to install Modernizr; however, this is not a straightforward process. There is no global `Mordernizr.js` file that lets you check every feature available in the target browser. Moreover, you have to build your (small) version of Modernizr yourself. Sounds complicated, but it really isn't. First, install Modernizr globally using `npm` via this command (you might need sudo rights):

npm install -g modernizr

Now, we can create the `modernizr-config.json` file that stores the modernizer configuration of our project. We set up the configuration file for SVG features; however, feel free to add more features to your configuration (check the available options via the link `https://modernizr.com/download` and click on **BUILD** to create your configuration file.

The Modernizr website

We create a configuration file for basic Canvas and SVG support as well as additional SVG features:

```
{
  "minify": true,
  "options": [
    "setClasses"
  ],
  "feature-detects": [
    "test/canvas",
    "test/svg",
    "test/svg/asimg",
    "test/svg/clippaths",
    "test/svg/filters",
    "test/svg/foreignobject",
    "test/svg/inline",
    "test/svg/smil"
  ]
}
```

Finally, we can build our custom Modernizr feature detection script using this command:

```
modernizr -c modernizr-config.json
```

You can also use the `-d scripts/modernizr.min.js` flag to change the installation destination of the Modernizr script to the `scripts` folder. Let's create an HTML document that includes this script:

```html
<!doctype HTML>
<html>
  <head>
    <title>Feature Detection using Modernizr</title>
    <script src="scripts/modernizr.min.js"></script>
  </head>
  <body>

  <script>
    /* here we go */
  </script>
  </body>
</html>
```

The preceding code shows how we included the Modernizr script on the page. Note that, besides using the command-line tool of Modernizr and the configuration file, you may also use a plugin for your favorite task runner (such as Gulp or Grunt) or simply download your custom build from the Modernizr website.

Using Modernizr in JavaScript

Let's try Modernizr's JavaScript API; it exposes all available features directly as properties on the global Modernizr object. Checking for SMIL support is as easy as the following code snippet:

```javascript
if (Modernizr.smil) {
  console.log('SMIL is available');
}
```

This is great; we can now easily check in JavaScript whether all our features are available and easily adapt the application and features to the target browser of the user.

 The complete list of available features is provided on the Modernizr website at `https://modernizr.com/docs/#features`.

Using Modernizr in CSS

Using Modernizr in JavaScript is great to adapt functions and scripts according to the features of the target browser. However, when we are dealing with HTML elements rather than JavaScript, we might want to use CSS classes to show and hide DOM elements based on the available features of the browser.

In the previous example, we added one option to the configuration file, which is called `setClasses`. This option adds classes to the HTML root node for every supported and unsupported feature. We can observe this by looking into the DOM tree of the demo page that is displayed in the following figure:

```
<!DOCTYPE html>
<html class=" canvas svg svgasimg svgclippaths svgfilters svgforeignobject inlinesvg smil">
 ▶ <head>…</head>
 ▼ <body>
   ▶ <script>…</script>
   </body>
</html>
```

The DOM tree of the website using Modernizr

In the preceding example, we see only the supported features named as classes on the root HTML node. Unsupported features will result in a class with a prefix called `no-`, for example, `no-canvas`, `no-svg`, and so on. Now, we can add CSS styles to our visualization to show and use available features or hide the unsupported functionality:

```
.no-svg .chart {
  display: none;
}
.no-svg .sorry-for-not-using-a-modern-browser {
  display: block;
}
```

In the preceding snippet, we remove the charts from the page and display an error message to the user that asks him/her to update to a modern browser. However, often we don't simply want to disable a functionality for a user on a non-compatible browser. Moreover, we want to add the missing functionality to the user's browser so that he/she can get a user experience that is similar to using the latest browser. Find out more about this in the following section.

We will use Modernizr class-based feature detection for the styling of our application more often than for detecting the SVG or Canvas support. Just think about a scenario where you want to animate some parts of your visualization using CSS3 animations. The advantage is clear; you will have the power of native animations in CSS instead of using manual timers and DOM transformations in JavaScript.

Therefore, we can include a CSS3-specific animation option in the configuration file, such as cssanimations, csstransforms, csstransforms3d, preserve3d, and more, and check for the availability of these features. Now, we can create native animations in CSS and create a fallback solution if CSS transitions are not supported:

```
@keyframes fadeIn {
  from {opacity: 0.0;}
  to {opacity: 1.0;}
}

.cssanimations .chart {
  animation-name: fadeIn;
  animation-duration: 4s;
}
```

As a JavaScript fallback solution, we add the following script:

```
<script>
  d3.selectAll('.no-cssanimations .chart')
    .transition()
    .duration(4000)
    .style('opacity', 1.0);
</script>
```

Naturally, we can also use the Modernizr JavaScript syntax, which is slightly more explicit:

```
<script>
  if (!Modernizr.cssanimations) {
    d3.selectAll('.chart')
      .transition()
      .duration(4000)
      .style('opacity', 1.0);
  }
</script>
```

We can now provide a trade-off between user-experience, compatibility, and performance for our visualization by adapting to the features of the target browser. Note that this trade-off comes at a cost—having multiple redundant pieces of code in your application that need to be tested and maintained.

Custom implementations of native features

There are three options for developers if a native feature is not available on a target platform or device:

* Drop the piece of code that uses the native feature

- Drop support for the browser that does not have the native feature
- Use a custom implementation of the native feature

Not using the feature at all is obvious and not the preferred way most often. Developers want to take advantage of modern browsers and their capabilities to provide better performance and best features.

Excluding some browser only because a tiny missing bit of native code is also frustrating. Don't get me wrong, I am not speaking about supporting IE7. New native features mostly arrive in one JavaScript engine first with a prefix (such as `moz`, `webkit`, `ms`, and more) before they are available across all modern browsers without prefix. This process usually takes a couple of years, and it's not guaranteed that all features will be implemented in all engines.

Polyfill – implementing missing features

We want to include native features without breaking the backward compatibility of our application to older browsers and different JavaScript engines. This can be done by implementing the native feature yourself in JavaScript and using it as a fallback solution whenever the native feature is not available—this is a so-called polyfill.

Note that there is, of course, a big difference of polyfilling different native functions with JavaScript. A polyfill for providing ECMAScript 5 compatibility by implementing array methods, such as `forEach`, `indexOf`, `map` and more, is much easier to include than a polyfill for the complete SVG 1.1 specification or the CSS Media Query specification.

A polyfill is usually a function that implements a native feature for a JavaScript engine that does not support this feature. If we speak in terms of supporting entire APIs, such as the previously mentioned SVG or Media Query specifications, we usually speak about abstraction layers rather than polyfills. Here is an example (slightly outdated): Internet Explorer 8 and lower versions don't support the SVG specification but their **own Vector Markup Language (VML)**. To use vector graphics in these browsers, you have to use an abstraction layer that provides a consistent API and generates SVG or VML, depending on the user's browser; RaphaëlJS would be such an abstraction for SVG.

 A list of popular polyfills can be found in the WIKI of the Modernizer project on Github at `https://github.com/Modernizr/Modernizr/wiki/HTML5-Cross-Browser-Polyfills`.

Shims – intercepting API calls

If you look for resources about cross-browser compatibility on the Internet, you will be confronted with many different terms that are all used in a similar way. Shim is one of these terms that is used very often in combination with polyfills.

A Shim is a general expression of a piece of code that intercepts a native API call — for example, a function — to provide a modified behavior of this function. This behavior can range from implementing the function, modifying the parameter list, and adapting the return values, to anything you can think of. Hence, a Polyfill is a Shim that implements the missing functionality of older browsers.

Wrappers – abstracting APIs

I need to apologize for speaking again about IE8 — this topic was very popular when SVG gained importance. Polyfilling the SVG API for IE8 would be madness and would often lead to incompatibilities. Therefore, it is much better to implement a Wrapper at the top of both APIs.

A Wrapper abstracts the behavior of an API, such as SVG, and provides a higher-level API to the developer. The goal is to be able to change the underlying technology of the wrapper to output for example VML instead of SVG in order to create cross-browser vector graphics without modifying the API for the developer.

Compatibility of D3

One might ask how compatible D3 is as a library; however, this question has no easy answer. D3 is a library for DOM transformations designed to use the underlying technologies such as CSS, HTML, and SVG. It is only the supporting framework that lets you access native APIs and features. Of course, the user is not forced to use SVG with D3 but could just as well use Canvas. The user can use only map projections, the event system, or scales. Therefore, we have to be a bit more general when speaking about the cross-browser compatibility of D3.

> Many of D3's internal features, such as scales, timers, colors, interpolations, and more, are available as extra packages on Github at `https://github.com/d3`. This comes handy when you only need a certain piece of D3's power for your application.

If you use D3, you will have to check the compatibility of the underlying technologies that you are using in your application. If you use D3 to manipulate SVG, you will have to check the SVG compatibility; and if you use the SMIL check for SMIL compatibility, if you use Canvas, and so on. You see where this is going.

If you just feel like using single pieces of D3 and are wondering about the compatibility of the internal core, then you have to check the compatibility of ES5 Array functions. The following screenshot shows the cross-browser support for ES5 in general. One can see that IE8 is the trouble maker:

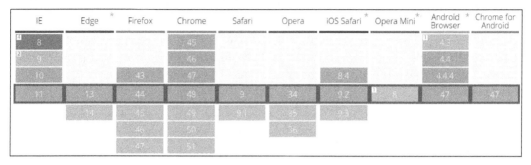

The cross-browser compatibility of ES5 (source http://caniuse.com/#feat=es5)

The recommended polyfill to use D3 functionalities in IE8 and IE7 (Heaven forbid!) is the Aight library, which mostly includes ES5 Array functions and APIs. The library can be found on Github via `https://github.com/shawnbot/aight`.

Cross-browser Media Queries

When creating cross-browser responsive visualizations, you will most likely have to deal with the Media Query support, measurement, and unit issues. The last two can be easily detected and fixed using Modernizr (cssvhunit, cssvmaxunit, cssvminunit, cssvwunit, and more) and fallback solutions.

However, fixing the Media Query support once it is not available is quite tricky. Why is that? If detecting the availability of Media Queries is quite easy (using Modernizr), polyfilling it is a big hassle. The main reason is that Media Queries usually occur in your CSS styles and not in your JavaScript code. Until now, you only learned that JavaScript functions and APIs can be polyfilled using JavaScript. So, if we would want a polyfill for CSS (it has to be written in JavaScript), it always has to parse the complete CSS document to extend its functionality. This means instead of the native styling performance, we will have to parse the CSS using JavaScript, apply all known styles, and fix new selectors, attributes, styles, and more and also apply those. This often leads to a suboptimal solution (performance wise).

Window.matchMedia() and its Polyfill

The JavaScript pendant of CSS Media Queries is the `window.matchMedia()` function. If this function is available, then CSS Media Queries are supported; if it's not available, we have to provide a polyfill for the function and fix CSS styles using the JavaScript polyfill.

In the following screenshot, we can see the support of the `matchMedia` function in different browsers. We can identify IE9 and Opera Mini 8 that are causing problems. Hence, if the application supports both versions, it needs to include a polyfill for `matchMedia`.

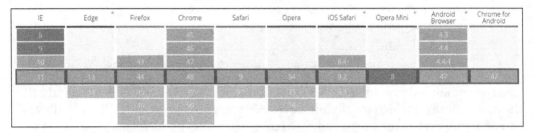

The cross-browser compatibility of matchMedia (source: http://caniuse.com/#feat=matchmedia)

You can install the `matchMedia` polyfill by downloading the latest source or using the bower package manager and running the following command from the terminal:

```
bower install matchmedia
```

Let's recall the following example from *Chapter 1, Getting Started with Responsive Design, Bootstrap, and D3.js*. Using the `matchMedia` function, we can apply some code only to certain device types in JavaScript:

```
if (matchMedia('screen and (max-width: 480px)').matches) {
  // user is on a smartphone
}
```

However, when we look at our style sheets, we usually find styles written in CSS, such as the following snippet:

```
@media screen and (max-width: 480px) {
  body {
    /* user is on a smartphone */
  }
}
```

As we have already found out in the previous chapter, we now need to use the `matchMedia` polyfill to add the Media Query functionality to CSS styles. The following sections will do exactly this.

Min-width and max-width support via Respond.js

We know what we have to do to polyfill Media Queries for CSS; we need to load CSS styles with JavaScript, parse them, find the Queries, pipe them through the matchMedia polyfill, and then style all affected DOM elements accordingly. This is exactly what the Respond.js library does but only for the min-width and max-width queries which are seen as the bare minimum feature set for responsive apps. Respond.js is written and maintained by Scott Jehl and available on Github at https://github.com/scottjehl/Respond. The following is a screenshot of the Respond.js test runner, which can execute in any browser and test the functionality:

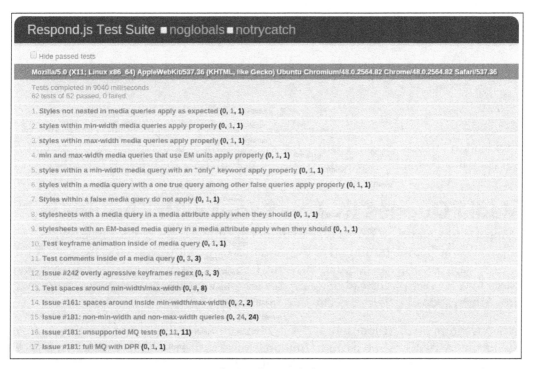

Respond.js Test Suite in the browser

You can install Respond.js by downloading the latest source or using the bower package manager and running the following command from the terminal:

```
bower install respond
```

Great! Now, we can set up `Respond.js` to automatically polyfill Media Queries (with all performance limitations). We simply have to include `Resond.js` after all included styles; it won't look for inline, imported, or styles linked after it was included. Here is a minimal layout using `Respond.js`:

```html
<!doctype HTML>
<html>
  <head>
    <title>Media Queries using Respond.js</title>
    <link rel="stylesheet" href="styles/responsive.css">
    <!--[if lte IE 9]>
    <script src="bower_components/respond/dest/respond.min.js"></script>
    <![ENDIF]-->
  </head>
  <body>

  </body>
</html>
```

In the preceding code, we wrapped `Respond.js` in conditional HTML comments to only load in Internet Explorer with versions less than or equal to 9. This doesn't affect our code in all other browsers and loads the polyfill only for Internet Explorer.

Media Queries in JavaScript with Enquire.js

Using Media Queries is a great way to define the dimensions of your responsive application as per the resolution of the target browser. However, whenever we want to provide cross-browser compatibility, the CSS file somehow has to be reloaded and parsed via JavaScript. Instead of doing this tedious reloading of resources, one can move the responsive styles directly into JavaScript.

When we implement responsive styles in JavaScript, we have to run functions once a Media Query matches and cleanup functions once a different Query matches. Hence, we want a comfortable solution to do so rather than using the raw match Media Query itself. The `Enquire.js` library by Nick Williams provides such an interface for registering Media Queries, callbacks, and clean-up functions. The source code is available on Github at `https://github.com/WickyNilliams/enquire.js`.

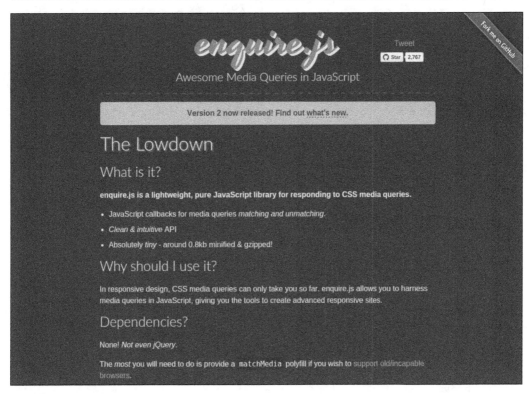

The Enquire.js website

You can install `Enquire.js` by downloading the latest source or using the bower package manager and running the following command from the terminal:

```
bower install enquire
```

Now, we can start defining our responsive styles in JavaScript rather than in CSS. This has the advantage that, in combination with the `matchMedia` polyfill, no other dependency is needed for compatibility on Internet Explorer. We provide only the responsive styles directly in JavaScript, which means there's no need to load and parse CSS files.

Let's create a little example where we use `Enquire.js` to hide a menu on mobile devices:

```html
<!doctype HTML>
<html>
  <head>
    <title>Media Queries using Enquire.js</title>
    <script src="bower_components/matchMedia/matchMedia.js"></script>
```

```
      <script src="bower_components/enquire/dist/enquire.min.js"></
script>
      <script>
        enquire.register("screen and (max-width: 480px)", {
          match : function() {
            // Enter smartphone mode
            document.querySelector('.menu').style.display = 'none';
          },
          unmatch : function() {
            //Leave smartphone mode
            document.querySelector('.menu').style.display = 'block';
          }
        });
      </script>
  </head>
  <body>
    <div class="menu">
      <ul>
        <li><a href="#">test</a></li>
        <li><a href="#">test</a></li>
        <li><a href="#">test</a></li>
      </ul>
    </div>
  </body>
</html>
```

In the preceding code, we used the match and unmatch functions to execute the callback, and we used the clean-up functions on the Media Query called screen and (max-width: 480px). This gives us full control of our responsive application, is only JavaScript and hence fully cross-browser compatibile (only if we include the matchMedia polyfill).

Cross-browser SVG features

We already saw in the previous chapters that SVG is only supported by Internet Explorer 9 and higher versions. Providing a complete cross-browser compatibility for the previous versions of Internet Explorer is not impossible but challenging. Theoretically, you can use a wrapper (for example, Raphael.js) to convert D3's output into the valid VML; however, this is tricky, difficult, and not a good solution performance wise. In this case, it would be even better to not use D3 at all for this problem as it will not give you additional benefits.

Whenever we spoke about SVG support, we were speaking about the basic SVG support and hence the SVG 1.1 specification. However, there are more interesting features that you can use in your application, where some of them have a different compatibility. Let's look at these features.

SVG animations

We have already talked about SMIL animations in the previous chapters; however, we want to bring it up again. Although compatibility doesn't look bad in the current browsers (if we neglect Microsoft browsers for a second), we need to be aware that SMIL will not be supported anymore in the future.

If you are going to implement SMIL animations (because they are easy and cool) you should also provide JavaScript fallback solutions for Internet Explorer, Edge, and Opera Mini:

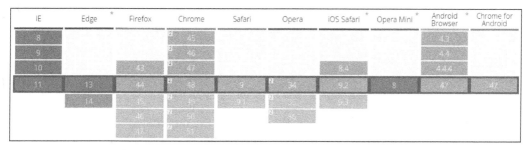

SMIL animations (source: http://caniuse.com/#feat=svg-smil)

If you are planning to animate elements along SVG paths using CSS (so-called motion paths), be aware that this is also not supported in many browsers:

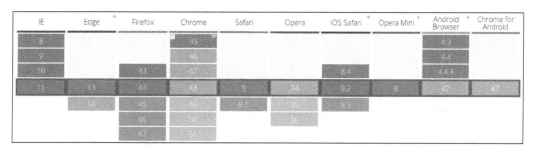

CSS motion paths (source: http://caniuse.com/#feat=css-motion-paths)

If you still want to animate elements along a motion path, you should use a non-native JavaScript approach. There is a great JavaScript function that returns a certain point on a custom path, giving the parametric length on the path; this is called `getPointAtLength()`.

More information about the SVG function `getPointAtLength` can be found on W3C at `https://www.w3.org/TR/SVG/paths.html`. An example using this function for implementing a path motion is available at `http://bl.ocks.org/KoGor/8162640`.

Using SVG filters

If you are planning to use filters in SVG, such as blending, blur, turbulence, and so on, you can go for it. Filters on SVG elements are supported in most of the browsers except Internet Explorer 9:

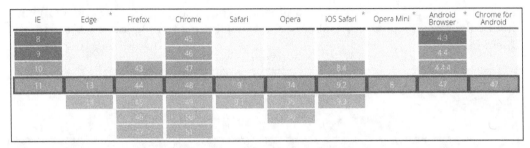

SVG filters (source: http://caniuse.com/#feat=svg-filters)

Just as with many other SVG features, they are also introduced to HTML elements via CSS. However, this will not solve our problem using Internet Explorer 9 but will only result in more restrictions.

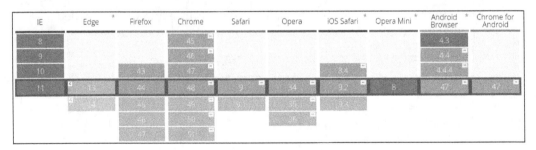

CSS filters (source: http://caniuse.com/#feat=css-filters)

To support image filters in Internet Explorer 9, I recommend using feature detection and the old deprecated DX filters.

 More information about DX filters can be found on MSDN at `https://msdn.microsoft.com/library/ms532853.aspx`.

Clipping elements in SVG

SVG lets a developer create elements that can be reused as clipping paths for other elements. Although this is a great feature, and I commonly use it in visualizations (I love clipping paths), this is not supported in all browsers. The following graphic shows the compatibility of the CSS property for clipping masks using the url(#id) syntax:

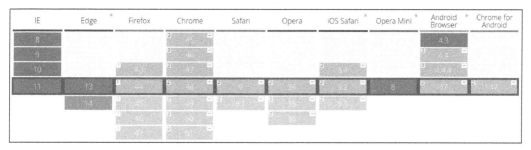

The CSS clip-path property (source: http://caniuse.com/#feat=css-clip-path)

Another drawback of clipping paths (and fill patterns) is this syntax; the element has to be accessible via the URL, ID, and the # hash symbol. I can imagine many scenarios where elements cannot be accessed via the URL and the hash symbol—for example, a single page applications that use the hash for routing. However, there exists no useful solution for this currently, and we need to rely on visualizations without clipping masks.

Handle touch and mouse events with ease

Until now, we have always tried to provide both touch and mouse events for users on a mobile device and on PC or television screens. With D3, we treated a touch event exactly as a mouse click event but only with a different interaction radius. However, it can easily happen that a user has both touch (or multi-touch) and a mouse as input devices. In this section, we solve caveats for developers when providing both input types for the user.

Mouse and touch events

Why could we use a mouse click event to also detect finger touches on a touch screen? To answer this question, we will take a look at the execution chains of events on a target DOM element mouse and go into touch-enabled device. We combine them into one execution chain for touching a target element on a touch device with the finger. Here is the list of events that will be propagated:

- `touchstart`: The fingertip touches the screen
- `touchmove`: The fingertip moves on the screen

- `touchend`: The fingertip stops touching the screen
- `mouseenter`: The mouse cursor is entering the element
- `mouseover`: The mouse cursor is hovering over the element
- `mousemove`: The mouse is moved over the element
- `mousedown`: The mouse button is pressed
- `mouseup`: The mouse button is released
- `click`: The element is clicked
- `mouseleave`: The mouse cursor is leaving the elements

By looking at the preceding list, many things become clear. For developing responsive applications, the preceding list will be your best friend when you deal with designing interactions.

The first thing we notice is that a simple touch with the finger will also propagate a click event. This explains why we can use the simple `click` listeners to detect both touch and mouse inputs. This is useful, and it will make the basic click functionality designed for mouse interaction available for touch interactions. However, make sure that you adapt interaction targets when implementing touch support.

The second most important insight of observing the execution chain is directly related with the first one. Whenever we support both touch and mouse events, we need to make sure that touch events don't propagate as mouse events in the execution chain. We will see in the following section how this works.

Another interesting insight might not be obvious from looking at the event chain. We observe that there is the `touchmove` event at the beginning and the `mousemove` event fires some events later. While this is true for a single finger tap, it is not true for a touch gesture when the finger moves on the screen. Unfortunately, when the finger is moving and firing the `touchmove` events, no `mousemove` event is propagated. This means that UIs designed based only on the `mousemove` events will not work properly on touch devices due to this behavior.

Breaking the event execution chain

As we have seen before, if one operates on browsers with touch input, the touch events are also propagated as mouse events. This behavior of the browser is called mouse-emulation handling and is enabled per default on every touch event. While this is a good thing, because it makes the mouse UI usable for touch devices even when no touch events are implemented, it slows down the performance when we actually use touch events.

There are many reasons why we would like to intercept the chain of fired events and default actions by the browser—to increase performance (as we just said), to disable scrolling when using the same gesture in a visualization, and to fully control the event chain.

JavaScript provides a function to disable the default behavior of the browser while maintaining the execution chain and propagating the event; this function is called `event.preventDefault()`. The default behavior of clicking on a checkbox toggling it, and the default behavior of using the mouse wheel scrolls the page. Whenever we want to prevent these default actions, we use the preceding function.

There is another function that does not affect the default actions of an event but stops the execution chain of the event; this function is called `event.stopPropagation()`. Whenever we want to stop event propagation, we use this function.

If you want to stop all event listeners for a specific event, you can also use `event.stopImmediatePropagation()`. This will stop all custom event listeners for a specific event.

> More information about `preventDefault`, `stopPropagation`, and `stopImmediatePropagation` can be found on MDN at `https://developer.mozilla.org/en-US/docs/Web/API/Event/preventDefault`, `https://developer.mozilla.org/en-US/docs/Web/API/Event/stopPropagation`, and `https://developer.mozilla.org/en-US/docs/Web/API/Event/stopImmediatePropagation`.

Touch events in D3

We previously saw that touchmove events don't propagate mousemove events. While both events seem to be identical (one used for mouse and one used for touch), there is a small difference. This difference will be very important to understanding why we should not simply use identical callback handlers that listen for both the events and execute the same function.

To understand the difference between these events, we simply think about their purpose. On Desktop computers, users often move the mouse cursor to reach a certain element on the screen. Therefore, the `mousemove` event is targeted to the closest element underneath the cursor, for example, the mouse is moving over an element.

However, a `touchmove` event happens intentionally on a specific element and can be seen like a `drag` (click and move with a mouse) event. The user aims to move a specific element. Due to the intention, the `touchmove` events are targeted to the element that was touched at the beginning and to the element that also received the `touchstart` event. While this seems to be a tiny difference in the specification of the `mousemove` event, it has a big impact on how to implement event listeners

Let's take a look at a little sample that implements a proper touch interface using D3. We draw a full-sized canvas on the screen and then process touch events on the canvas; this can be the start of a small drawing application:

```
<svg class="drawing">

</svg>
<script>
$canvas = d3.select('.drawing')
    .attr('width', document.body.clientWidth)
    .attr('height', document.body.clientHeight);

$canvas.on("touchstart", touchstart);

function touchstart() {
  console.log('Touch started');
  d3.event.preventDefault();
  d3.select(d3.event.target)
    .on("touchmove", touchmove)
    .on("touchend", touchend);
}

function touchmove() {
  console.log('Touch moving');
  d3.event.preventDefault();
}

function touchend() {
  console.log('Touch ending');
}
</script>
```

In the preceding application, we register the `touchmove` and `touchend` events directly on the target of the `touchstart` event. This is a nice trick, so we don't have to worry about a static target of these events. In the following screenshot, we can see how touch events are emulated in Chrome to test this small sample application:

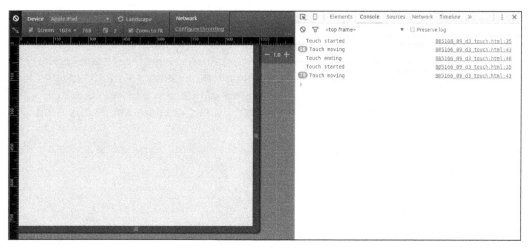

Touch Events emulated in Chrome

However, when using events with D3, we need to make sure that they don't propagate through the full execution chain and result in mouse emulation. As we already saw, events are stored globally in the `d3.event` object when using D3. You can still stop the execution chain of the events and prevent default actions using the `d3.event.preventDefault()` and `d3.event.stopPropagation()` functions.

A note on detecting Touch Devices

In the first section of this chapter, we heard about feature detection and Modernizr. We can simply evolve these thoughts and argue that it should be rather easy to detect devices with touch support and maybe offer a different user experience to touch devices than to desktop devices.

While detecting touch support is rather easy and straightforward, there is no way of detecting touch devices. We can either check if the `touchstart` event is available, if it is working properly, we could check the device width, and so on. In the end, it doesn't matter because there are no classical touch-only and mouse-only devices anymore. There are Android tablets with connected mice, convertibles with touch and mouse, laptops with touch and trackballs; the list goes on. You will quickly realize that it doesn't make any sense to categorize these devices into touch and non-touch.

Therefore, my advice is to never implement a feature for touch and another feature for mouse interactions rather than implement an interaction that can be used with both mouse and touch (and even pen).

A hover state for touch

We will quickly realize that, when dealing with touch and mouse support, the application state needs to be adapted. A very common case for these states is the hover state, which can be achieved by hovering over an element with the mouse pointer. The following figure shows a typical application of the hover state in a visualization; it reveals more information about the current position by hovering over a data point:

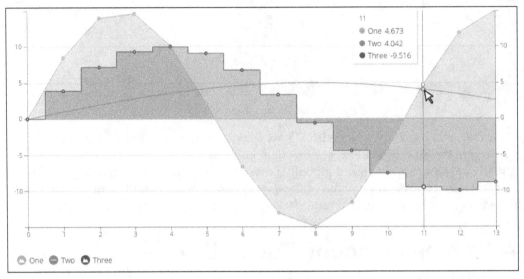

A Hover interaction

While this is a great use of the current mouse pointer position, this state doesn't (usually) exist in only touch devices. Hence, we need to modify this behavior such that even touch devices can access this information. We previously read that detecting touch devices is impossible, and therefore, we cannot simply add a button for touch devices but should instead rethink the interaction.

In the preceding example, we can implement a cursor that we can drag from an axis into the chart. This might not be a perfect replacement for hover states, but it brings us on-track to the new interaction model. We can now argue that a hover event (or a simple tap) on the chart reveals a cursor at this position (or the closest data point). Practically, it is exactly the same interaction as before; however, we now have to also think about how to remove the cursor from the visualization—maybe by moving it back onto an axis. I hope you get the idea; by rethinking the interaction, I mean exactly this—thinking about where the hover state (or tap) can still work and enhance the new interaction by implementing and optimizing the interaction for touch devices from beginning to end.

If you want to support both touch and mouse events, you might be better off dropping the hover feature completely and replacing it by a different interaction. The reason why we often have problems doing this is that the `:hover` state is a valid CSS selector, and hence it can implement many nice features via CSS rather than JavaScript.

However, if you cannot let go of your hover state, you add the `focus` state (which is also a valid CSS selector) to every `hover` state. This ensures that a single tap on a touch device shows the information as the mouse cursor in the hover state. The following example shows the difference between the hover (left) and hover + focus (right) states; I encourage you to open it with your touch devices and play around (the source is provided with this book):

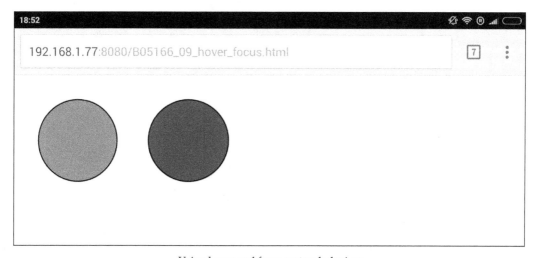

Using hover and focus on touch devices

 Note that in some browsers, a click also triggers a hover state (this is different to the JavaScript execution chain of events though); therefore, the hover state will work just by tapping in some browsers on touch devices

Pointer events – combining mouse, touch and pen

Browser vendors realized that only emulating mouse events on touch events is not enough to solve the problem of multiple interaction devices. Therefore, W3C came up with an abstraction layer on top of all pointing input devices and wrote the pointer events specification.

The idea is simple, as shown in the following figure, all pointing input devices should not be treated separately (by separate events) but instead be combined into a single input device called Pointer. Developers would then implement support for pointer events and hence automatically provide a great UI for all the types of pointing devices.

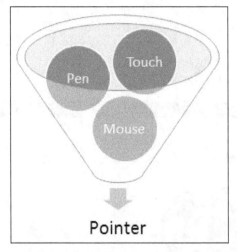

Pointer events (source. https://www.w3.org/TR/pointerevents/)

While this sounds amazing and a great step towards multiple pointing input devices, the browser vendors are not very keen to implementing this specification. A quick look in the cross-browser compatibility chart (see the following figure) reveals that the specification is currently not usable:

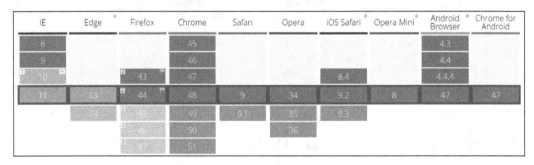

The cross-browser compatibility of Pointer Events (source: http://caniuse.com/#feat=pointer)

While you might be disappointed now and ask why I am teasing you by bringing this pointer event thing up, I believe that in the future browsers will support this abstraction for pointing devices. However, be aware that, with Apple's ForceTouch, new interaction possibilities will emerge that may require separated treatment. While supporting these features on separate device types for an enhanced user experience, treat the Web as a common place for user-friendly, accessible and multi-platform applications.

 More information about pointer events can be found on MDN at `https://developer.mozilla.org/en-US/docs/Web/API/PointerEvent` and the W3C website at `https://www.w3.org/TR/pointerevents/`.

Disabling pointer events for elements

For completeness, I also want to mention the `pointer-events` CSS property that should not be confused with the previously discussed pointer events. This property can be used to disable pointer events (hence mouse, touch, and more) on a DOM element. While this was part of the SVG specification already, it is now also supported on HTML. The following figure shows the complete cross-browser compatibility:

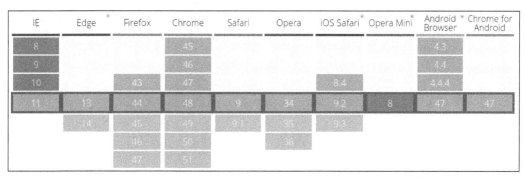

The cross-browser compatibility of the pointer-events property
(source: http://caniuse.com/#feat=pointer-events)

The `pointer-events` property is useful whenever you want to block an element from receiving events, such as overlays or partially overlaying elements, or whenever you want to make sure that proper elements receive events on touch devices.

Let's look at a simple example with overlapping circles:

```
<style>
    circle.focus:hover, circle.focus:focus {
      fill: rgba(0,0,255,0.5);
    }

    .all-events {
      pointer-events: auto;
    }

    .no-events {
      pointer-events: none;
    }
  </style>
<svg class="drawing">
  <circle class="focus" r="35.9" cx="50" cy="75" />
  <circle class="all-events" r="35.9" cx="50" cy="50" />
  <circle class="focus" r="35.9" cx="150" cy="75" />
  <circle class="no-events" r="35.9" cx="150" cy="50" />
</svg>
```

In the preceding code, we set the first overlapping `circle` element to receive all events properly, whereas the second does not receive any events. In the resulting application, we can now easily click the second underlying circle, whereas the first one is very hard to click due to the overlapping element. Here is a screenshot of this example:

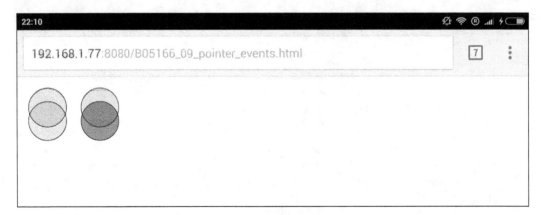

The Point-events property

Summary

In this chapter, you learned how to solve the most common cross-browser issues with the best tools. With Modernizr, we can build a lightweight script that detects supported browser features in CSS and JavaScript. We can provide polyfills or use a wrapper whenever it is necessary.

For creating an SVG visualization using D3, we need to be aware of the restrictions from the supported SVG specification. Hence, we need to take special care when dealing with filters, animations, and clipping paths.

You learned how to create responsive visualizations that work across all browsers. One key thing to remember when using Media Queries is the `matchMedia` polyfill, which is commonly used by other tools to polyfill the native JavaScript function. `Respond.js` is a great polyfill for simple CSS Media Queries, and `Enquire.JS` motivates you to move your Media Queries to JavaScript.

Finally, we discussed different mouse- and touch-related problems and a solution for building cross-browser compatible applications for both mouse and touch. Now, you are prepared to implement great responsive visualizations using one of the best visualization libraries out there: D3.

I hope you enjoyed this book; it was a pleasure for me to share some of my passion and expertise with you. If you are happy with this book or have any questions, remarks, or feedback, please contact me on Twitter at `@ChrisiKrnr`. Happy coding!

Index

Q

Queue.js
URL 172

R

Raster/Pixel Graphics
with canvas 22, 23
Real Devices
syncing, Browsersync used 190
Regular Expressions
in JavaScript, URL 69
relative lengths
conclusion 86
using, in SVG 84-86
remote data
any string data, parsing 67, 68
dates, parsing from strings 70, 71
loading 64-67
numeric values, formatting 72, 73
numeric values, parsing 72, 73
parsing 64-67
strings splitting, Regular Expressions
used 68-70
require.js
URL 100
Respond.js
max-width support via 215
min-width support via 215
reference link 215
responsive applications
remote debugging 193-195
responsive charts
about 83
JavaScript resize event, using 93
relative lengths, conclusion 86
relative lengths, using in SVG 84-86
viewport, scaling 87-90
Responsive Design
%, REM and EM 6, 7
about 2
breakpoints 4, 5
conditional CSS, with Media Queries 2-4
Mobile Devices, designing 7
viewport 6
responsive events 108

S

SASS format
URL 99
SASS precompiler
URL 8
Sauce Labs
URL 201
scales
creating 47
data values, mapping to pixel range 47, 48
linear scales, for linear mappings 48
ordinal scale, for mapping non-numeric
data 48, 49
time scales, for mapping time-series
data 49
selections
URL 31
semi-automated tests 183
shapes, drawing
about 42
arcs, drawing 46
areas, drawing between curves 45
lines and curves, drawing 42-44
shape tweens 149
shims
about 212
API calls, intercepting 212
SMIL Animations
URL 126
**solutions, to cross-browser compatibility
issues**
conditional comments, for Internet
Explorer 204, 205
D3 compatibility 212, 213
native features, custom
implementations 210, 211
native features, detecting with
Modernizr 205-208
sphere
projecting, on flat map 154
spherical Mercator projection 166
stopImmediatePropagation
reference link 223
stopPropagation
reference link 223

SVG (Scalable Vector Graphics (SVG)
  about 2
  animating, Synchronized Multimedia
      Integration Language(SMIL)
      used 124-126
  clipping elements 221
  filters, using 220
  Vector Graphics with 24-26
  shape abstractions, URL 42
SVG animations
  about 219
  reference link 220
SVG elements
  Data Binding and Dynamic
      Properties 35, 36
  data-driven transformations 34
  manipulating 33
symbol maps 173-175
**Synchronized Multimedia Integration
    Language (SMIL)**
  used, for animating SVG 124-126
system tests 183

T

Test-driven development (TDD) 185
testing
  about 180
  and debugging 187
  automated testing 196
  automated tests 183
  continuous Integration 185
  in Cloud, running 201
  integration testing, Protractor and
      Selenium used 199-201
  integration tests 184
  manual testing 186
  manual tests 182
  need for 181
  on local machine 196
  semi-automated tests 183
  strategy, for visualizations 202
  types 182
  unit tests 184
  unit tests running, Karma used 196-199
  visualizations 180

TopoJSON
  about 160, 161
  to GeoJSON, via Client API 162
  URL 161, 162, 175
  via Server API 161
touch devices
  detecting 225
touch events
  about 117, 221, 222
  event execution chain, breaking 222, 223
  handling 221
  hover state 226, 227
  in D3 223-225
  touchmove 221, 222
  touchstart 221
transitions
  about 139-141
  attribute and style tweens, for
      custom interpolation 143, 145
  chained 145-148
  path transitions 142, 143
TravisCI
  about 185
  URL 201

U

units
  for absolute lengths 80
  for relative lengths 81, 82
  for resolution 82
  in browser 80
  mathematical expressions 82, 83
unit tests 183, 184
Update Pattern
  URL 41
  using 40, 41

V

Vector Markup Language (VML) 211
Vector Graphics
  hardware-accelerated Pixel Graphics,
      with WebGL 24
  in browser, with SVG 21
  Raster/Pixel Graphics, with Canvas 22, 23
  with SVG 24-26
viewport 6